Shingling The Fog
And Other
Plains Lies

Shingling The Fog And Other Plains Lies

ROGER WELSCH

SAGE BOOKS

THE SWALLOW PRESS INC.
CHICAGO

First Edition

Sage Books are published by
The Swallow Press Incorporated
1139 South Wabash Avenue
Chicago, Illinois 60605

This book is printed on 100% recycled paper

ISBN 0-8040-0545-1
LIBRARY OF CONGRESS CATALOG CARD NUMBER 75-171876

For Fred Kirchhefer, a Wyoming Job.

CONTENTS

CONTENTS

Shingling The Fog
And Other
Plains Lies

INTRODUCTION

I said in my haste, all men are liars.
Psalms 116:11

. . .an experienced, industrious, ambitious, and
often quite picturesque liar.
Mark Twain

Several years ago at an academic conference I sat quiet-
ly boiling as a man who purported to be an important
frontier historian declared that there had been little cultural
interaction on the northern Great Plains frontier because
"there was no time for telling stories or singing songs." During the discussion period following the lecture, I opposed
his contention, but I realized nonetheless that his point of
view is a widespread one. Indeed, if this well-read scholar
believes that the subsistence struggle of the pioneer necessi-
tated a moratorium on traditional culture, then it seems altogether likely that the general public, less sophisticated after
all in folklore and history, should believe the same thing
But he was wrong. The Eskimos who live in a life-long
struggle just to scrape together the basic materials for existence have their songs and stories. The Australian Abori-
gine in his desert environment crafts a simple musical in-
strument when he could be making weapons, sings when he
could be hunting, carves images of wood and stone when he
could be digging roots for supper. Was the settler of the
Great American Desert then so preoccupied with survival
that he had no time for culture, for amusement, for songs
and stories?
Well, actually that is the wrong question—because it is

based on a false premise: that culture is a thing apart from, even opposed to, the processes of life and survival. It is not a matter of finding time for songs, stories, and art apart from the normal activities of hunting, building, fighting, procreation. The Eskimos' music is not mere entertainment; it may serve as a litigation action, as a social announcement, as a proclamation of love. Primitive art is not a diversion from the day-in, day-out hunt; it is frequently an integral part of that hunt. It is a mistake to look for decorative folk art only outside the world of pioneer practicality; Plains folk art is to be found as a functional component of subsistence—the patchwork quilt, for example, imposes man's drive for color and pattern (that is, art) onto a very functional form, which could have been put together much more simply and quickly without the added quality of artful design.

Songs, art, and tales cannot therefore be viewed as segments apart from life processes. This mistake leads to the additional mistake of viewing these traditional materials as alternatives to the essential activities of subsistence, and then to the dichotomous point of view that the arts, oral and material, traditional and sophisticated, are antitheses of man's pragmatic, vital struggle for life.

On the Plains one cannot ask how the pioneer found the time, energy, and courage to sing and tell tales, for that is a nonsensical question: the songs and stories were a very essential element of the pioneer's struggle. The strength of his arm and the craft of his mind were two other essential components, but without the strength of spirit exhibited, encouraged, and communicated through tales and lies like those in this collection, the homesteader for all his muscle and brain was defeated. The success of his trial was not at all *in spite* of the time he spent laughing but rather *because* of the time he spent laughing.

Nor, for the same reason, are these exaggerations of the hardships of the Great American Desert designed to be in-

sults. These stories were not the property of those who painted on their wagons, "In God we trusted, in Nebraska we
busted. Gone home to live with the wife's folks"; they were
constantly circulated by those who stayed here, those who
loved the prairie and learned to live on it, with it. That they
seem to many "boosters" to be scurrilous attacks is a result
of the naivete and romantic nearsightedness engendered by
chamber-of-commerce thinking. I love Nebraska too, and I
find great excitement in what she was and is—but not in what
she might be. The pioneer felt that he gained no credit from
growing a crop in a garden; his' accomplishment was growing a crop in a desert. Even today there is a certain pride
enjoyed by those who have attained some goal by conquer-
ing hardship or surviving a disaster, and, conversely, there
is disdain for those who coast by on the bounty of the rich
land or a kind providence. So the homesteader magnified
the perversity of his chosen land to magnify his own achieve-
ment in overcoming those hardships, and he converted the
agony to humor in order to make the actual burden seem
lighter.

Certainly part of the problem the modern Plainsman has
in understanding the mentality of the pioneer is the radical
change in Plains geography. As I point out throughout
this collection, in many cases the difference between the truth
and the lie of the situation was not as dramatic as it might
be today. Even now Europeans and travelers from the eastern United States are unprepared for what they find on the
northern Plains. If in this day of worldwide and immediate
communication the Norwegian is amazed by the vast tree-
less stretches of Cherry County, what must have been the
amazement of the uneducated, frequently misinformed homesteader of 1860, when there were far fewer trees, even along
the rivers, and slower transportation made the distances
seem even more vast. For that matter, I suspect that even
some Nebraskans would be surprised to know that today

the great square bordered by U.S. Highways 20 on the north and 83 on the east, and State Highways 27 on the west and 2 on the south encloses nearly 6,000 square miles *untraversed by a paved road*. On one occasion I was trying to get to a farm north of Whitman to examine a barn, and after struggling along simple rut roads for nearly an hour, I had to give up—finding out later that the farm is fifteen miles off the nearest *graded* road and cannot be reached except by horse, airplane, or four-wheel-drive vehicle.

The newcomer to the Plains must have been as dazzled by geographic truths as he was by the lies. Who after all could believe tales about the incredibly vast, table-smooth stretches of Dakota prairies, the Black Hills gold, endless herds of great wooly buffalo, the mile-wide-inch-deep Platte River, grass fires moving across the tips of sun-dried blades faster than a man could ride on horseback, the Devil's Cattletrap near Scottsbluff where huge jelly-like blisters of slimy clay lay quivering, able to swallow a man or horse. It was here that the New American often first encountered Indians, cactus, sage, rattlesnakes, and desert drought. It is with good reason then that one folklorist entitled his article, "So-Called Tall Tales About Kansas," for "the Kansas stories are for the most part factual with only a little exaggeration; the similar stories told in other places are mostly exaggeration with a little truth."[1]

It is of course difficult to assess the importance of the tall tale and lie within the entire inventory of pioneer Plains folklore, but it is certainly my impression that they constitute a very substantial proportion of the entire corpus. They are the most predominant survival of pioneer folklore into the present; the old-timer who has forgotten the songs and longer stories will still recall a few of his favorite lies. In my *Treasury of Nebraska Pioneer Folklore* (1966), a collection of materials gathered during the Depression years by the Federal Writers' Project, a substantial proportion of the body was also tall tales; *Kansas Folklore*, edited by Bill Koch and Sam Sackett, suggests about the same importance of the tall tale in that state. That tall tales were popular enough to constitute a successful commercial advertising device also suggests a degree of currency (see my comments about Febold Feboldson in the chapter entitled "Big Men"); and response to my "teaser articles" in the *Omaha World-Herald's Magazine of the Midlands*, in which I asked readers to send me pioneer tall tales and lies they recalled, has been far greater than answers I have received in regard to "teasers" about other types of pioneer Plains folklore.

An examination of the Notes at the end of this book will show that a good number of the tales in this collection came from the *Nebraska Farmer,* and this perhaps deserves some explanation. It can also tell us something about the distribution and form of the tall tale during another period on the Plains. In the December 6, 1924 issue of the weekly *Nebraska Farmer*, there appeared for the first time a column entitled "The Liars [sic] Lair," with the subheading, "A Prize Contest to Determine Who Is the Champion Liar of Nebraska."

A description of the tall tale and lie as "folk lore" dealt with the differences between ordinary exaggeration and the traditional tale, and an example was given, as provided by Ralph Snyder, president of the Kansas State Farm Bureau:

"An Illinois man, having been in this country but a short time, wrote to his brother who was to follow later: 'Don't come! This is the most atrocious climate you ever saw. As I was driving to town yesterday one of my oxen died from sunstroke. Before I could get him skinned, the wind turned to the northwest and froze the other one to death.'"

It was suggested by the editors that the stories not be more than 150 words in length, nor less than 50, but it was clear that this lower restriction was generally ignored by both the writers and the editors. By way of a prize, the editors offered "a medal which says that you are the Champion Liar of Nebraska." (They continued, "Maybe you already are, but only your wife knows about it.")

The next week, in the December 13, 1924 issue, the column appeared again, urging readers to submit their entries to the tall-tale contest. Again, by way of example, the editors included a story which had been "told" to them "the other day":

"The same cyclone in Seward County that performed the remarkable stunt of turning a gallon jug half full of water wrong side out without cracking the jug or spilling a drop of water, a few years ago tore the tin roof off of a concrete silo. The next morning when the stacks of hay and stray horses had settled down to 'terra cotta' again, the farmer found the tin roof neatly rolled up in one corner of the yard. The roof was guaranteed for ten years, and so the farmer promptly shipped it back to the factory in Detroit.

"Two weeks later, he received a letter from the manufacturer of a light automobile of popular make, made in that city, who had apparently received the roof by mistake, reading as follows: 'We have repaired your car and are shipping it back to you under separate cover today. The repair charges of $11.80 will be cancelled if you will tell us how your car ever got into such terrible shape.'"

The contest lasted until the end of February, 1925. The editors urged on the liars of the area by giving weekly awards of almanacs and describing in glowing terms what an honor it would be to wear their prize medal for "the state championship in lying, the greatest of all winter sports." Some entries came in dedicated to George Washington, causing the editors to comment, "Someone has said that it certainly was not Washington, D.C., who never told a lie."

As should always be the case in any liars' contest, the editors, on the last day of the contest, decided to extend the deadline, thus lying about the contest itself. They also announced on February 28, 1925 that they had such a backlog of lies and stories that they would continue to publish the column and that they would also welcome any additional contributions readers might like to send in.

The column received mixed reviews from the newspaper's readers. The following is representative:

"To the *Nebraska Farmer:* I am not one of those fellows to say, 'I told you so,' but I knew your contest would fall flat. In the first place, your paper put the appeal to the wrong class of people; farmers are not liars as everyone knows. And in the second place, it is the wrong time of the year; the farmers are too busy figuring up their income tax and they never think of lieing [sic] when they are doing that. You should have waited until the women folks got their incubators all set and with nothing to do but sit around and wait for them to hatch—then you'd have had some real lies from the women folks!"

The man was a prophet. Women dominated the lying, in contrast to my field experience, and the first-prize winner was also a woman, Mrs. J. A. Milliken of Aurora, Nebraska:

"If I could wear your prize meddle on my buzom I would be the happiest man in this great common-weather—but I cannot tell a lie!

"Allow me to relate a natural Phenomization I saw back east fifty years ago. One afternoon a whirlwind swept into our yard, struck the bee hives and played swing your pardners right and left with the bees. Then it spun the windlass of the well around like the crank on a jitney and followed the bucket and rope right down into the well. When that whirlwind reached the bottom it shot the bucket sky-high and blew the water out with a roar only to fall a second later like a mighty cloudburst.

"Pa found the old windlass blowed chuck full of bee stingers drove porcupine fashion right into the wood. The well was bone dry and has never freshened since. Finally the county commissioners pulled the hole up by the roots and sawed it into lengths for road culverts. The bucket was standing by the overturned bee hive and was full of clear strained honey.

A sack of flour that had been in the kitchen was up in a tree, but the sack was gone.

"Yours for the hole truth, Mrs. J. A. Milliken."

"The Liars Lair" continued, but appeared only irregularly beginning in April of 1925; the last of the series appeared in the May 16, 1925 issue. But during those few months the weekly column had recorded nearly seventy-five tales, most of them clearly traditional and still in circulation today.

It is not my intention to suggest that the tall tale and lie of the sort of version included in this present collection are exclusive to the Plains or were first derived here. Collections from other states—in fact, from other parts of the world—contain many of the same stories.[2] But the ones here are Plains (and particularly Nebraska) folklore to the extent that all occur in the area and therefore constitute a loose Plains corpus. A naive, dilettante critic once attacked one of my publications of Nebraska folklore because some of the materials can also be found outside the state boundaries; of course, folklore has very little respect for political lines of demarcation. If I were to discover some item of folklore that had never crossed a state (or county or city) border, I would have to question its legitimacy as traditional folklore, for if it were indeed a part of the living body of materials in traditional *circulation* (the touchstone of true folklore), how could it have avoided crossing some boundary or another, unless it were artificially promulgated—thereby, by definition, disqualifying the material as folklore. No. These stories are not exclusively Nebraskan or northern Plains property. The same stories can be found in other collections—*but in differing combinations and forms.*

I have attempted to present the stories and lies here as I heard them or found them. Those collected from oral sources were frequently picked up on street corners, at social gatherings, over barbed wire fences, or after lectures at the foot of the podium. Therefore, the wording itself is often based on my memory and is not intended to represent a precise transcription. Those texts sent to me in letters are reproduced virtually word for word. My intention in doing this is twofold: first, I hope by such accurate reproduction to preserve the stories more reliably for future studies that might be able to use them; secondly, I find that a substantial part of the attraction of the stories and lies is in their simple form and salty diction.

I have referred to the stories collected here as both lies and tall tales. Few of them have the well-developed narrative elements associated with tales, yet all of them have at least a hint of narrative content. Settling firmly on either name would carry the sense of the free mixture of various elements apparent in this material.

The lies, even when they are presented as narrative tales, are usually short. Many are only a simple statement. An examination of the motifs (see Motif Index) shows a predominance of the disregard of logic or some physical fact. Actual or pretended detail is frequently inserted by the narrator to lend an air of truthfulness to the lie, which is not to say that there is any real attempt to foist off the lie as truth; it is only a part of the ingenuous, straight-faced delivery of the lie—as if the teller himself believed it.

And when these lies are told orally, they are done so without laughter, with a straight face. They are usually told by men (a clear contradiction between my experience and that of the editors of the *Nebraska Farmer*). They are often told in an exchange sequence, each liar trying to outdo the last, but never laughing at even one's own tale. During such exchanges, there may be a silence between the stories, as if the audience were pondering the wonder of the event just described—but the pauses are more likely opportunities to recall even more amazing tales. The stories are frequently localized or personalized, embellished with the actual names of persons or places, specific designations of time and number, to bring the lie even closer to the form of a truth.

Although many of the lies followed traditional paths of diffusion into the northern Plains, moving in with immigrants from the East and from Europe, others were most certainly inspired by peculiar features of Plains geography, which is so dramatically different from that east of the Missouri.

Finally, while my interest here is primarily in pioneer tales, it must be noted that the tall tale and lie are by no means merely survival elements of tradition. Many of the following chapters conclude with lies that are quite recent in development and dissemination. Last week, while visiting a friend in Colorado Springs, I heard his twelve-year-old son tell a story (without really understanding the joke) about a man "who is so tall that he has to stand on a chair to tie his necktie," and this morning's paper carries the following item:

CHAMPION LIAR IS LIED ABOUT BY LIARS CLUB
Burlington, Wis. (UP) We can't swear the following story is true. The Burlington Liars Club said it has reached an ultimate of sorts for an organization of its nature—it lied about the world's champion liar.

The club had said earlier that A. Wunderwald of Pura Ti, Switzerland, had won the contest for saying it was so cold in his hometown in August that "sable furs ran after ladies."

But the club then said the real winner was Danny Tomovich of Rosemead, California, who said, "Our town is so strict about litter laws that anyone will be fined $50 for telling a dirty joke."

At least that's what the club said he said.[3]

So the tradition of the tall tale and lie is not a dead one; here I am only discussing examples from some earlier stages of this great and honored occupation, "the greatest of all winter sports."

ROUGH WEATHER

1

Now Hurrah for Lane County, where the
    blizzards arise,
The wind never ceases and the moon never
    rises,
Where the sun never sets, but it always remains
Till it burns us out on our Government claims.

Traditional Plains folksong

The weather is always doing something there;
always attending strictly to business; always
getting up new designs and trying them on people to see how they'll go. But it gets through
more business in spring than in any other season. In the spring I have counted one hundred
and thirty-six different kinds of weather inside
of twenty-four hours.

Mark Twain

Everybody talks about the weather, but no one
does anything about it.

Charles Dudley Warner

I have lived in Nebraska now for thirty-odd years and so
it was no surprise to me that when I had finished taking notes
for this collection the fattest stack of cards stood behind the
marker labelled "Rough Weather." I cannot imagine that anyone ever gets used to Plains weather. And it is in this category that one really has to sympathize with the honest man,
for his dedication to honesty in reporting Plains weather will
make him out to be the grossest kind of prevaricator. What
could I possibly do to convince my friends in the East that
it is quite true when I tell them about the year we had a
shirt-sleeve picnic on the hills above the Platte River one
December 19th—and then could not get out of the driveway

the next morning because of the snow drifts. I am not sure I myself believe any longer the time some of my colleagues and I went tobogganing one morning, lightly sweatered flew kites in the early afternoon, and finished the day by hauling out our sailboats for a pleasant sail under the hot late afternoon sun. I have seen it rain and snow out of a crystal-clear sky, the sun shining as if it did not know any better. I have been in a car stuck in a dust drift which had formed across the road. A few nights ago the weatherman reported that the high temperature for the day in Grand Island, Nebraska had been 2° and the low 1°. Last week I drove eastward across the entire state of Nebraska and I crossed the Lancaster County line wondering where all the snow reported over the radio had gone, only to find when I arrived in Lincoln, ten miles later, that I had to spend several *hours* digging away the huge mounds of snow in my driveway. It has probably been said of every township and state in America, but never with more truth than when said of the northern Plains, "If you don't like the weather here, just wait a few minutes."

In describing weather here it hardly seems worth the trouble to lie. The largest hailstone recorded in the United States fell at Potter, Nebraska, on July 7, 1928; it weighed one and one-half pounds and had a diameter of 5.41 inches. Daily temperature increases of as much as 40° and 50° have been recorded—and hourly increases of 20°! A reading of −47° has been recorded in Morrill County, Nebraska, and 118° at many locations, including Hartington, Nebraska—an absolute range of 165°.[1]

In his *The Sod-House Frontier,* Everett Dick says that on November 15, 1871, the children ran barefoot and plowmen had to stop frequently during fall plowing to rest their teams in the face of the unseasonable heat. The next morning they awoke to find the windows covered by huge drifts of snow. The blizzard battered the Plains for three days and two

nights; in Lincoln the weather bureau recorded a temperature of −17° and a seventy-mile-an-hour wind.[2]

Mrs. Lillian Grush of Salem, Nebraska put her thoughts
and experiences with the vagaries of Nebraska weather into
doggerel verse for the *Nebraska Farmer*'s "Liars Lair" (for
which the editors, incidentally, awarded her that week's prize,
"a handsome grain-leather gravy ladle"):

> Of all the old grannies a fellow might find,
> Our State beats them all for changing her mind.
> It may be quite warm and there comes a big freeze,
> Or it may be quite breathless and comes a great breeze.
>
> I was mowing the sunflowers out around the medder,
> I let down the bars, turned the cow in and fed her.
> The air was so breathless one breath had to do
> Where I had been in the habit of taking two.
>
> As I was trying to drive in the geese,
> Along came a breeze and stripped off their fleece.
> I grabbed up a sack and caught every feather.
> Says I to myself, "This is wonderful weather."
>
> When I went to the house, I just had to stare,
> For I found it was whirling around in the air.
> 'Tis a truth I am telling, by thunderation,
> It lit hind side before on the same foundation.
>
> And as it was whirling around in mid air,
> The old cow blew into the basement where,
> As the critter fell, she shook out her milk
> In the separator tank, just as fine as silk.
>
> The breeze it turned that darn old crank
> Just as sure as my husband's name is Hank.
> And I dreamed as I slept on my brand new feather,
> There's nothing can beat this Nebraska weather.[3]

WIND

Pioneer accounts and interviews never fail to mention somewhere the ferocity of winds on the Plains. One of the primary advantages of the sod house was that the hot summer winds and cold winter winds penetrated its three-foot-thick walls only with great difficulty and one of the primary disadvantages of the soddy was that those same winds could lift the roof and throw it into a ravine several hundred feet away.

I was once examining the construction of a barn while a north wind cut through the barn and my coat, making it nearly impossible to even think clearly about what I was supposed to be doing. "No wonder the wind blows that way," chattered the farmer, who had accompanied me out to the barn to see that his white mare did not bite me (which she did anyway). "There's nothing stands in its way between here and the North Pole except one little cedar tree about two miles this side of Winnipeg."

Very much the same sentiment was expressed by a hotel keeper when E. C. Spooner, who had just arrived in this country, asked ". . .if the wind always blew this way." "Oh no," he said, "sometimes it blows real hard. This is just a spring zephyr." Later Mr. Spooner asked him ". . .what was beyond those hills." His answer was, "More hills."[4]

A fellow folklorist in Indiana once asked me why Nebraska barns never have wind vanes, when east of the Mississippi almost all barns do. I passed the question on to a seasoned farmer, who replied, "No sense to it. When you want to see which way the wind is blowing, you just look out the window and see which way the barn is leaning."

To the same question, another told me that his father did develop a Nebraska wind vane: he bolted a twelve-foot logging chain to a stout post set well into the ground and then he could tell the wind direction by watching which way the chain was blowing. He noted, "We could tell the wind was really blowing when links began to snap off the end of that chain."

My brother-in-law, Ed Henry, recently met an Ohioan, who commented when he found that Ed was from Nebraska that he once had a friend in Nebraska, who ". . .never had to hang up his hat; seems he just put it up against the wall and the wind held it there."

I once asked a member of Nebraska's Blizzard of '88 Club, an organization made up of veterans of that famous storm, if he could remember anything about the blizzard. He said that he was just a boy at the time, but he could remember that ". . .the wind was blowing so hard that it took four strong men just to hold a blanket over the keyhole of [my] father's sod-house door."

Good old American ingenuity in one such case transformed this problem into a household convenience. An old bachelor harnessed the sand blast which ripped through his kitchen keyhole, holding his pots and pans in it until they were spic and span.[5]

A Federal Writers' Project report noted another application of pioneer ingenuity to the sandstorm phenomenon—which would have been a problem to the less clever. A Chadron, Nebraska newspaper, commenting on a sandstorm that swept the town in 1900, said that at least the storm had one advantage. All the town carpenters had to do was place a board lengthwise in the gale and in just a few minutes it would be sandpapered to the finest surface."[6]

An anonymous writer told me about having seen a log-chain wind vane with links snapping off the end and then continued, "But the wind is not really blowing 'til it raises the dust so high that the road you are travelling on is so up in the air that you have to look down to see the traffic signs, which have been blown ahead from so far behind that you think you're travelling in reverse and shift gears and back up to the end of the wind and drop fifty feet into your own backyard." He commented with remarkable accuracy, "Nebraska is known to be a pretty windy place—in more ways than one."

This is reminiscent of the report in the *Lincoln State Jour-*

nal in the "Dirty Thirties" of a duststorm and its consequences: "A man and his wife, returning to New Mexico from the east, drove 200 miles in a circle in the storm, refueling three times in Elk City, Oklahoma."[7]

H. E. Schievelbein, a friendly old-timer with a fine inventory of stories, has some particularly interesting ones about the wind:

"Once during corn planting time the wind blowed so hard when Dad got ready to go to the field in the P.M. he hung the sack with about one-half bushel of seed corn on a nail on the side of the granary and after he had the horses out of the barn and ready to take off for the field he went back for the sack of seed corn and be darned if the wind hadn't ripped the sack off the nail and left the seed corn hanging there."[8]

"Our chickens had about all the feathers ripped off, especially the long tail feathers, and we had a small stack of cane bundles left over from the year before and one old hen had made a nest on top of this hump of cane, and laid her eggs on top every day. One day when the wind was real strong she was on the nest with her vent facing the wind, and be darned if she didn't have to re-lay that egg five times before there came a lull in the wind so that she could get off the nest. The wind would always blow it right back in her vent when she thought she had it laid."[9]

M. J. Krebs of Antelope County had wind trouble with his cattle in much the same way. Seems that he could not keep them fed because the wind blew the hay out of the cattle as fast as they could stuff it in.[10]

But one man's misfortune is another's advantage. After one particularly bad windstorm ". . .a farmer continued searching around to see if there was anything he could salvage. He went to see how his pigs were and was pleased to find that they had enough air blown into them by the wind that they were plenty large enough for market."[11]

According to a report in the *Lincoln State Journal*, the

winds continued to blow with this kind of ferocity well into the twentieth century; a horse that was left tied to a tree over-night, a *Journal* article said, was found hanged the next morning, the wind having blown away the sand on which he was standing.[12]

Another correspondent said, "My parents told this one. It happened in 1896. On June the 5th a tornado in Howard County [Nebraska] moved a church—Our Lady of Mount Carmel—off of its foundation. The next week another big wind set it back on. They didn't call it a tall tale—just a miracle."[13]

And finally, this magnificent example of "verifying detail": "One day Dad noticed a tumbleweed piled up among many, many others in a plum thicket in a canyon and it had a cardboard tag wired on with baling wire. Dad dug it out from among the others and on one side of the tag was some writing: 'Am turning this weed loose April 17th. Finder get in touch with me please.' Name and address, but names slip my memory: 'Rosebud, South Dakota.' On the other side someone had wrote, 'Discovered your weed in a three-pronged fork of a cottonwood tree April 18th. And since the wind has shifted, am sending tag and weed back on the same route. Hope it finds its way back.' The weed showed considerable wear. Don't recall the name, but the address was Arapahoe, Oklahoma. Dad notified the man he had found the weed but it was wore so tread-bare and no way to re-tread it, he burned it along with a whole stack of others." The teller, otherwise so full of helpful facts and details, does not bother to mention that the weed had travelled something over 500 miles in one day![14]

And those "zephyrs" were as unpredictable as they were powerful and fast: One day a farmer saw the same tumbleweed blow by his house three different times, going in three different directions.

Speaking of tumbleweeds, it might be appropriate to mention here another of those true facts that seem closer to fiction. I was doing a study of Nebraska pioneer buildings made of baled-hay—which seems incredible enough, I admit —when I received a letter telling me about one settler's laconic solution to his tumbleweed problem: "I do not know of any [houses] made of hay but my folks bought a farm 9 miles west of Bridgeport, Nebraska, in December, 1912. It had a sod house on it and lots of tumbleweeds in the fence rows, so my father had a hay baler, so he baled the tumbleweeds and made a good-looking two-room house out of them."[15]

A large group of Plains tall tales deal with much the same theme:

"During the 'dry thirties' a farmer decided to build a fence. One day he drilled a half-mile of postholes. During the night a strong wind came up and blew away all the top soil. When he went back the next day, all he had was a half-mile of postholes standing on top of the ground."[16]

A former colleague at Dana College in Blair, Nebraska, Bill Thompson, once told me very much the same story, but he added that the worst part of the situation was that the wind blew those postholes across a great field of cactus and poked them so full of holes that they would not hold dirt anymore.

In "So-Called Tall Tales About Kansas" an informant tells about one such instance where the holes at least did not go to waste: they were fetched out of the ravine where they were blown and were driven into the ground for a well.[17]

And if it was not one thing, it was another: "Holes? My grandfather had a well 200 feet deep, but the gravel around it was sandy and a windstorm blew it away and left the hole up 200 feet in the air. He had his sons-in-law saw it up and they used it for fence-post holes."[18]

To a similar story the editors of the *Nebraska Farmer* remarked, "This was a great deal better than buying his postholes from a mail-order house as is so commonly done where the ground is too hard to dig them."

It may seem strange to those who have never lived on the

Plains that the wind should blow so hard, but it does sometimes seem that the prairie winds have a mind of their own
—and a sense of humor:

"On one occasion we had a corncrib filled with 500 bushels
of ear corn. In the north side of the crib was a knothole.
The wind blew one ear of corn at a time through the knothole, shelling the corn as the cob went through. When the
wind went down we had a crib filled with shelled corn and
the cobs were piled up outside."[19]

It stands to reason that Kansans would suffer from the
same sorts of wind troubles, since, after all, that cedar south
of Winnipeg is also the only thing that stands between *them*
and the North Pole. It is said that letters to one particular
Kansas town had to be addressed to Nebraska during the
summer because the wind would blow the town and its citizens north of the border. But in the winter the situation was
rectified: the winter northern wind blew the town back into
Kansas.[20]

A similar situation developed during the great dust storms
of the 1930s when a check by surveyors disclosed that the
state line had been blown a mile and three-quarters east.[21]

In *Kansas Folklore,* Mary Frances White has a story about
a tenderfoot who unknowingly opened his mouth during a
Kansas windstorm and swallowed about six or seven bar-
rels of air. The previously slender fellow was blown up like
a pin cushion, four or five times his normal size. When he
jumped from the wagon, he bounced along like a tennis ball
for about three miles, where he finally lodged in a canyon.
"It was a week before he was back to his normal size."[22]

At least one source suggests that the perverse winds were
not really native, but just might have been imported along
with the windy immigrants: "Incredible as it might seem, the
wind blew down the stovepipe into the stove, so that it turned
one of the covers over to get exit. This heavy iron cover was
about seven inches in diameter. When we put it back, the
stove rattled until again the cover was turned over. Jimmy

O'Brien said it was an 'Irish Tornado'—that the wind blew 'straight up and down.'"[23]

TORNADOS

Tornados and their tricks are known around the world, but according to the evidence of pioneer tales their frequency and playfulness is especially evident on the northern Plains. Not content to drive straws into trees and carry hats for distances of fifty or sixty miles, these mischievous twisters turned crockery jugs inside out, blew the hair off a man's head, played the trick mentioned above of pushing corn through a knothole in a corncrib, turned 200-gallon cisterns inside out, and even picked up a seventeen-mile stretch of Missouri Pacific railroad track with a train on it, turned it completely around without disturbing so much as a tie, rail, or spike, and then set it down again, so that the passengers and crew were amazed to find themselves arriving in Wichita, the town they had left less than an hour before.[24]

Tornados could pull the water up out of a well and leave it eternally dry, take apart a hive of bees and strain out the honey, pluck chickens, remove a man's socks without disturbing him otherwise in the least, and—one of my favorite of all tornado pranks—move a fence carefully to the top of a row of cottonwoods so that a breachy cow that had climbed through that fence for years had to climb up one side of the trees and down the other to get the job done the next day.[25]

Field workers for the Federal Writers' Project in Nebraska found early newspaper reports about a tornado that "turned a well inside out, a celler upside down, moved a township line, blew all the staves out of a whisky barrel and left the bunghole, changed the day of the week, blew a mortgage off a farm, blew all the cracks out of a fence, and knocked the wind out of a Populist!"[26]

A corresponding informant told me about one pioneer's close call with a tornado: "One of my favorites of all [of my father's] tall stories was about one of his neighbors who lived close to Republican City, Nebraska—Old Republican City, that was covered up with water from the Harlan Dam. This neighbor saw a tornado coming and not having a storm cellar handy, took refuge in a small depression in the ground where a tall telephone pole also stood. As the tornado came closer the neighbor was picked up by the wind and raised to the top of the pole. As the tornado passed he was lowered back to the ground unhurt, which makes for a pretty tall story, don't you think?"[27]

Any man on foot on the open prairie had to think fast when a tornado caught him by surprise. One man, for example, was carried into a tornado along with a pig. To keep from dropping to the ground and being crushed by the fall he "grabbed the hog by the tail and shoved him out of [the tornado]. Down we went for about a hundred feet, and then I pushed the hog back into the cyclone. I kept on doing this, dropping about a hundred feet each time, until the hog and me were back on the ground again."[28]

In a *Prairie Schooner* article, George L. Jackson tells as verified facts some of the pranks of early Plains twisters. In "Cyclone Yarns"—tornados were called cyclones in pioneer times—he says:

"April 30, 1888, a cyclone passed over Howard County, Nebraska. This cyclone was not of the mass of windstorms but was a whirlwind with personality. The idiosyncrasy of this twister was its avidity for water. Every well, stream, and watering trough that happened to be in its path was sucked dry of its moisture and left as parched as the Sahara. Some wells were dry for weeks; the water in the creeks flowed into the dusty sands never to be seen again; even the cows for several days gave never a drop of milk."[29]

"On July 12, 1900, a cyclone with distinct uprooting proclivities passed near Onowa, Iowa. Trees, grass, corn, alfalfa, every form of vegetation in its path was uprooted and left, for the most part, in tangled heaps and windrows. Striking exceptions were noted. One old oak had been uprooted without a leaf or twig being injured, carried through the air and balanced upright on the roof of a barn over two miles away. Twenty bird's nests were counted in the tree but not one egg or a fledgling had been disturbed."[30]

According to Jackson and his informants, the perverse tornados were not an isolated phenomenon; they spread their peculiar kind of prank over a broad region:

"On the 18th of May, 1916, a man near Scotland, South Dakota, had just put the finishing touches on a garage in preparation for a new Ford that he intended purchasing when one of the typical midwest cyclones appeared on the horizon. After the passage of the storm he emerged from his cyclone cellar and was surprised to find in his garage a brand new Buick bearing a Kansas license plate."[31]

Jackson even has one tale from the southern limits of the Plains:

"On June 6, 1912, a cyclone passed near Stilwell, Oklahoma. One of the early settlers in the community had dug a wide, deep well and had curbed the walls with pieces of native rock. Misfortune dogged the steps of the pioneer until the point was reached where the mortgage was due and he was about to be dispossessed, when the cyclone crossed his place. The 'twister' pulled up the old well as a derrick would lift a straw and carried it several hundred feet where it was left firmly planted but upside down near the farmer's barn. He plastered it inside and out and he used it ever since as a silo. From the old well gushed a geyser of oil. The farmer now has a summer home in the Adirondacks and a winter home in Palm Beach."[32]

Anyone who has tried to count the rich farmers or oil wells in Oklahoma knows better than to doubt that story, but I feel that the next one is likely to strain the imagination of even the most charitable audience:

"Joe Kucera reports a narrow escape that he once had

when a cyclone hit his sod house. The storm turned the sod house end for end on the same foundation without spilling any water out of the water bucket, and the next morning he found himself in bed in the kitchen with his underclothes on upside down and buttoned in the back."[33]

Sometimes tornados were rather cruel in the practice of their pranks:

"Keith Wallace, of Graden County, sends the following cyclone story: 'One of the funny things that a recent cyclone did in this community was to blow our chicken house away. After the storm, we all ran out to see about the chickens and found the only rooster we had in a half-gallon jug with his head sticking out, crowing, and not even a crack in the jug. We had to break the jug to get him out and found the handle on the inside of the jug.' "[34]

Sam Dahl, of Nebraska Wesleyan University, recently told me that a cousin of his "was once practicing his tuba when a Nebraska tornado came along and screwed him twelve feet into the ground. "[35]

In Kansas the great funnel clouds that every spring come sweeping up from the southwest did their share of peculiar damage, like bending the steel beam of a plow back between the handles without moving the plow from where it had been left in the field. But like Jesse James the twisters also seemed to have a soft spot in their hearts for the poor pioneer farmer: one such tornado seized a plow left in a field and plowed a farm for a pioneer woman who had been recently widowed; another helped two men who wanted to exchange houses but keep the same land by switching the houses—moving even the wells and cellars; and a third helped a new settler by taking the materials he had gathered and building him a house—right down to digging the cellar, laying the bricks, mounting the windows so carefully that not one was broken, painting the completed house (including of course the trim), and then even having the good taste to visit the local art shop, pick up some appropriate paintings, and hang them neatly on the walls.[36]

Like virtually every feature of Plains weather, each extreme is balanced and matched by its precise, and equally annoying, opposite. So it is also with the wind. There is apparently no such thing as moderation. One blistering hot Nebraska summer the wind never blew, not a breath, leaving settlers gasping for air. In fact, it is said, the situation became so desperate that the state legislature passed a bill restricting windmills to one per township since there was just not enough wind to turn more than one at a time.[37]

CHANGES

In the introductory remarks to this chapter, I commented on the incredibly rapid change of weather on the Plains; this feature of the geography did not escape the attention of the storytellers:

In Kansas a farmer walked over to a well to get a bucket of water for his oxen, which were suffering terribly from the heat of the day. But by the time he got back to the wagon, one of the cattle had died. He looked around to his bucket and the weather had changed so quickly to the north that his bucket of water had frozen to solid ice.[38]

The changes were so abrupt, indeed, that they could actually be seen coming, and the consequences were sometimes disastrous:

"I was riding the range one bright October day. The sun was bright and it was uncomfortably warm. Suddenly a blizzard broke and I started for the ranch as hard as the horse would go. For the full five miles it seemed as though we were riding neck and neck with the front edge of the storm. My face was warm from the sun and the summerlike day, while cold blasts from the blizzard were chasing up and down my spinal column. When we got to the ranch, the horse's neck and shoulders were covered with foam and lather while his rump was covered with snow and his tail was frozen so stiff that it came off a few days later."[39]

Sometimes mention of these weather changes, so much a part of normal pioneer life, are mentioned only in passing while telling of other events:

"Every day we hear about the man who started to chase a deer when he was cultivating corn and had to run him into a snow drift to catch him."[40]

COLD

During any one season in Nebraska it is impossible to imagine the existence of its diametric opposite: spring and autumn are so glorious that one is necessarily convinced that this climatic paradise is eternal, but since these seasons are seldom more than a few hours long, the idyll never really gets a chance to set in. Under a blistering July sun, the human mind is incapable of admitting that there could be a winter, and, on the other hand, during head-splitting January cold no imagination can conjure up memories or anticipations of July in its agonizing magnitude. So, if you are reading this during the summer, leave off trying to imagine what winter was and will be like, because your psyche will not permit it. Just keep these few stories in mind and in January they will be called daily to mind.

Newspaper editors in the 19th century had a way with the language. They considered themselves wits, even if their readers admitted only the half of it; in their editorials they treated not only the issues of the day but also the fine points of the news that might otherwise escape their readership. Mari Sandoz, who had a sensitive eye and ear for folklore and popular culture and used it tenderly and effectively, reported a particularly brutal blizzard:

"The Hays Spring paper admitted a slight chilliness of 38

degrees below zero, but nothing comparable to Rushville, where a leg froze off a cast-iron heater and the thermometer dropped to the lowest point ever recorded in Siberia, one degree above Gordon [Nebraska]. "[41]

That may have been the winter when, so one informant told me, "it got so cold. . .that they had to dig down twenty feet into the ground just to read the thermometer. "[42]

Anyone who doubts that it really did get cold might be interested in a few examples of the results:

"I remember the blizzard of '88 and many other cold winters. Many a time we had to use a ladder to get up on the roof to chop off the smoke clouds that had frozen on the chimney. "[43]

And yet another:

"It got so cold in some of the soddies that the fire froze on the candles and they had to bury them to get it dark enough to sleep. "[44]

And if that was not trouble enough, in Kansas, once the thaw set in, the flames that townspeople had broken off the candles and lamps and thrown outside thawed out and started minor fires all over town.[45]

"The first thawing days of spring were filled with train whistles and sounds of trains going by, the sounds of which had frozen and thawed out only when warm weather came. "[46]

The same informant went on:

"The winters were long and cold. I once set a pitcher of water out to cool. It froze so fast that the ice was warm. "[47]

A North Dakota sufferer recalled that it was so cold it was taking undertakers a full week just to drive corpses into the ground with a pile driver.[48]

Everything froze, and sometimes it got to be too much for a man:

"A storm had broken in November and [I] had hurried home, built a fire, put on the coffee pot, and lit the kerosene lamp. Suddenly there was an explosion. The steam had fro-

zen in the spout of the coffee pot until it burst. Next my fire
went out; the smoke had frozen solid in the pipe and smoth-
ered out the fire. I decided to go to bed, but when I went to
blow out the light I found the blaze frozen so hard it could
not be extinguished. I left early the next morning, fearing
that real winter might set in. "[49]

On a similar occasion J. O. Lobb noticed "his brother's
words freezing. . . , he caught some of them in a sack, and
carried them home and thawed them out by the fire. His in-
ability to catch them all resulted in a disconnected line of
chatter that he could not understand. This happened during
the winter of the 'blew' snow in Missouri. "[50]

"During an extended cold spell. . .a local editor received a
first-hand report from [a preacher] on how cold it got at
Split Log in Newton County. [He] wrote that one morning
he was sweeping the snow off the front porch and it seemed
so frigid that he decided he'd just find out how cold it really
was. So he leaned his broom against the side of the house,
went in and brought out a thermometer and hung it from
the top of the broom handle. 'Well, I can tell you, I really
got cold when I came back out in about 30 minutes and the
mercury in that thermometer was halfway down that broom
handle.' "[51]

That thermometer must have been inferior, because one of
my storytellers says that the mercury in his thermometer
jumps up and down in the bulb to keep warm.[52]

And today, January 21, 1970, as I was working on this
study, the announcer of a local radio station reported that
it was so cold last night that the "red stuff" in his thermometer
turned blue.

When man suffered on the Plains, his animals also felt the
agony:

Miss Odetta Brust "noticed that her mule team, standing in
the barn, never ate their hay nor even their grain for several
days. Finally she investigated and found that they had frozen to death standing up in perfectly lifelike positions. "[53]

An informant wrote me, "The cold weather stories remind me of an incident years ago. One morning was so cold that when my dad went into the chicken house, he found our rooster with seven inches of frozen crow sticking out of his mouth. "[54]

And the depredations of that winter weather could recur at unusual and unexpected times:

"Floyd B. Holcik of Kimball County recalled one bitter, cold day in '89 when the mercury was sucked right down into the bulb on the thermometer and then froze and bursted the bulb. Mr. Holcik and his hired man were talking about the low temperatures and their words froze as fast as they were uttered. The next spring, on the first warm day, the frost came out of the talk and the words began to thaw. The hired man was absent minded and imaginative and after listening for a moment or two he began to shiver, and in two minutes he was frozen to death. "[55]

I was once telling some of these stories and lies in a Grange meeting in Blair, Nebraska, and after I had finished my part of the program, an old fellow with a snowy white, full beard came up to me and said, unsmiling, that all this talk about the cold winters reminded him of the winter when he looked out his farm house window on an exceedingly cold morning and saw two cottontails pushing a jack rabbit —trying to get him started.

A poet identified only as "H.E." commented on the length of Plains winters—and in the same quatrain struck out at the summers:

> Nebraska's clime is very nice—
> If you are fond of snow and ice;
> This goes for nine months of the year,
> The other three you fry and sear.[56]

HEAT

It is not at all surprising that the newly-arrived homesteader suffered from the heat, since even the animals that had developed in this country suffered:

"One real hot day I observed a coyote and a jack rabbit in our pasture; evidently the coyote had been chasing the jack rabbit and as it was so hot, the coyote's tongue was almost dragging on the ground and they were both just walking. The coyote was perhaps twenty-five or thirty paces behind the jack. Wonder if the coyote ever caught the jack."[57]

One summer heat story was without question the most widely known and it is still the one the field worker hears most frequently today:

"A farmer was plowing corn with a team of mules. It got so hot the corn began popping. The mules thought it was snow, so they froze to death."[58]

A Kansas variant of the same story has the farmer capitalizing on a similar situation with predictable American ingenuity. Not only did his popcorn pop on that hot day, but his cane also melted, and ran down the hill into the corn, forming one huge, sticky mess of popcorn balls, which the farmer sold for 5¢ each, and did quite well at it.[59]

"Hot? It was so hot here in Nebraska that a lot of *stoves* burned up!"[60]

"It must get fairly warm in Gosper County too if what Cora Van Boskirk of that county says is true; and it must be true or she wouldn't have written it. The cows in that county give pasteurized milk. They become so hot during the blistering daytime and then cool off so suddenly when the sun drops out of sight that the milk is processed within the cow just as it is done in the big vats in the city dairies. (Of course this would not work if the farmer would milk before the cool of the evening, but they have been too busy to do the milking before dark for so long that it is impossible now to get near a cow to milk her without carrying a lighted lantern.)"[61]

In fact, from all evidence, the Plains may be the hottest place on earth, and Nebraska may be the hottest place on the Plains:

"Three farmers all died the same time. All of them wanted

to be cremated. One was from Texas, one from Kansas, and the third from Nebraska. The guy from Texas was ashes in two hours — ditto for the Kansan. But when they left the guy from Nebraska in two days, they opened the door and he jumped out and said, 'My God, two weeks more like this and there won't be any corn crop this year.' "[62]

This is clearly contradictory to other reports we hear about Texas. How can we ignore the statement of the man who said that if he owned a store in Texas and a house in Hell, he would sell his business and go home?

The other states have not been heard from yet, and no real conclusions can be drawn until all evidence is in, as this one tale from Arizona suggests:

"It gets so hot in Arizona that the farmers there feed cracked ice to their chickens to keep them from laying hard-boiled eggs."[63]

DROUGHT

Again the mind boggles at the truth of the matter. According to Everett Dick, "From June 19, 1859, until November 1860, not one good rain fell and there were but two slight snows in winter in Nebraska."[64] The northern Plains were known in those days as The Great American Desert, not because people were stupid or naive, but because it fulfilled in every way their conception of the desert — a vast, desolate, hostile waste, inhabited only by nomadic tribes. The fact that the sand was covered with grass was irrelevant; there was also the cactus. Modern rain charts were not a part of the pioneers' consideration, for *they* knew drought when they experienced it. Today, when we think of "desert," we think of the Sahara or the Mojave, but the pioneers did not know the Sahara and the Mojave; this was their desert, and the fact that it is now a rich farmland obviously could not be a factor in their minds, just as we cannot weigh in our minds today the consideration that the Sahara and Mojave may some day in the future be made fertile or be made to appear insignificant in their hostility next to the deserts of Mars and the Moon.

It was dry. Sometimes, it is said, pioneer children were ten years old before they saw rain and then it frightened them so that they would run and hide under the beds to escape this frightful, unknown thing. Public schools started training programs to ease the problem, poking holes in the bottoms of cans and running water through them to give the children an idea of what rain might look like.

"A stranger asked if it was really as dry here as the rumors had it. An old timer replied, 'Well, do you know your Bible?' 'Yes,' the stranger replied. 'Well, do you remember the story of Noah?' 'Yes.' 'Well, the same year he had his forty days and forty nights of rain, we had about a quarter of an inch here.' "[65]

Drought, like all other hard weather, took its toll on man and beast alike:

"It was so hot and dry for so long our hogs developed cracks between the ribs, like an old wooden barrel setting in the sun without water in it, and as there were some spring-fed water holes along the creek which used to run through the old homestead, it was my chore to drive the hogs down to the creek twice a week and let them wallow in them water holes several hours in order for them to soak up so they would hold a slop."[66]

Harry Chrisman, a distinguished western historian, wrote me: "I fully realize it would be a serious impediment to my work as a historian should I win a Liars' Contest. . . .However, since what I am about to relate is absolute truth, I feel the judges will realize that what I am doing is simply recording weather history of Custer County, Nebraska. . . .

"This occurred during the dry days of the 1930s. At that time I was motoring one day from Bassett to Broken Bow and midafternoon found me along a very poor and sandy road west of Westerville. My wife was with me and as we drove along at a speed of perhaps 30 miles per hour in the twin ruts that passed for a farm road, I observed a skunk a few rods ahead, and on my wife's side of the car. As we approached, I warned her to quickly close the car window, though the heat was stifling. She managed to get the window rolled up just as we came alongside the skunk. It quickly flipped up its tail, stood on its front legs, and blasted away at us. To my amazement, as I passed by I observed just a spray of *dust* emanate from the animal, much like the old-fashioned powder from an El Vampiro container, which we used in the earlier days to kill flies. As I mentioned, this was during the drought period of the 1930s, and this animal was so dehydrated there was not an ounce of moisture left in its body."

And an anonymous informant in Aurora, Nebraska told me that around there frogs had grown up to be seven years old without having learned how to swim.

During the dry summer of 1878, it got so dry on the Plains that "when the fish swam up the creek they left a cloud of dust behind them,"[67] and some farmers had "to run their wells through a wringer in order to get enough water to cook with."[68]

Another tale came to the *Nebraska Farmer* by way of mere mention in a letter addressed to their complaint service:

"To the Protective Service Department: I have a neighbor who is terrible mean, and I'd like to have you help me collect damages from him, or advise me what I can do. It was this way:

"Last fall we had a little twister here and it tore out my well. (I live in a canyon.) It hoisted the well up on the divide and set it up on end, upside down. The well was 200 feet deep. Now the land up there is owned by Dick, and what did he do to pester me but dive up to the bottom of my well and bore a little hole in to let the water squirt out over my place. It is naturally pretty dry here and so, in falling so far, the moisture is pretty well dried out of the water by the time it hits the farm. As a result my cows have been giving condensed milk all winter, and the hens are starting to lay powdered eggs. One of my great troubles now is that the wife doesn't like to wash clothes in evaporated water and it is hard to churn butter out of condensed milk. Now, what I want you to do is to tell me how I can make Dick let me go on his land and get my well again. Please help me. This is a terrible how-do-you-do for me to be in!

"Yours thankfully, Hans Hansen."[69]

A Nebraska settler heard during a particularly severe drought that one of his neighbors was finally surrendering to the elements and was pulling up stakes. He found the disillusioned homesteader standing on the roof of his sod house pouring a bucket of water over the parched sod. "What are your doing up there?" asked the sympathetic visitor.

"Well, ever since I built this thing eight years ago, I've wondered if the roof would leak and it's never rained enough for me to find out."[70]

There are many tales about farmers being able to carry their year's harvest to market in their pockets. A Lincoln friend once told me that his grandfather used to recall how he on one occasion stopped to visit a drought-stricken family in their soddy. He asked the farmer if crops were really as bad as they seemed. The farmer, chewing on an ear of roasted corn, answered, "For lunch we just et four acres of corn."[71]

Some farmers feared that the only crop one could raise in this country was taxes, but it was not just for themselves that they felt sorry:

"A farmer with his son met another ragged farmer on the main street of town one day during a particularly bad drought season. 'Looks a bit like rain,' the one opined hopefully. The other replied, 'Well, it doesn't matter much one way or the other to me; I've *seen* rain. But,' he went on, pointing to his teen-age son, 'the boy here. . . .' "[72]

A Kansan who was not to be outdone by stories of Nebraska weather told me that it got so dry sometimes in northern Kansas that when the ground cracks opened up to their widest it took two men to see all the way to the bottom.[73]

This report is verified by yet another Kansas story of deep ground cracks. Seems a farmer's dog fell into one and in his efforts to locate the dog the farmer dropped a logging chain into the crack. The next morning, when he returned to renew his rescue efforts, he could hear that chain clanking as it was still falling.[74]

DUST

The natural result of all that wind and drought is dust. During the dust bowl years, people in Lincoln would awaken to find everything coated with a film of red dust—from Oklahoma or Texas, for there is no red dust in eastern Nebraska. Southern farmers threatened to bring their plows up north, since a good half of their farms had settled there.

Thomas Henry Tibbles, writing about early days in Nebraska, quoted a settler who commented about an approaching, ominous dust storm, "Prices out here are subject to violent fluctuations. This is only a sudden but general rise in real estate."[75]

Prairie dogs and gophers seem to have been especially discomfited by dust storms:

"I remember in the thirties a dust storm so thick that a salesman saw a prairie dog twenty feet above the ground digging like hell to get back to earth."[76]

"Dust? It had been so dark all day you couldn't see, but toward evening I saw a ray of sunlight. Investigation showed a gopher had blown up with the dust and dug his way back down and the sun was shining through the hole."[77]

And when they were not confusedly digging their way down

through the dust, they were trying to get above it all:

"In the 1880s there was once such a thick dust storm that all the prairie dogs in the state thought they had been buried. They dug up through the dust storm to get out and for three hours after the dust had settled it rained prairie dogs."[78]

One of Wyatt's informants reported that a driver once got his car stuck in a mudhole and when he returned he couldn't find his car anywhere because it had been obscured by a dust storm.[79]

White has a similar but much more complicated version of the event. During a dust storm it began to rain, but the water could not make its way through the dense dust, and so it collected on top of the storm. Among other strange things that this caused: a windmill, which was sticking above the dust into the water, was pumping dust out over the top of the whole mess.[80] One wonders how this situation was ever resolved.

PRECIPITATION

" When it rains, it pours" is a frequent and bitter proverb on the Plains. One farmer, answering my comment about the weather never seeming to be right for farming, said, without humor, "If we didn't have bad weather, we wouldn't have no weather at all."

In reading early accounts of sod-house life I have found frequent references to flash floods that swept down otherwise parched canyons to sweep away a homesteader's soddy and all his meager property. Stories are rife of soddy dwellers awakening late in the morning to find the room still dark, the windows having been covered with drifted snow. Others tell of the doors of their soddies being blocked by huge drifts, which meant that they had to tunnel out, if the door opened in, or wait for the thaw or dig out through the ceiling if the door opened outward.

"It used to snow so bad that the snow-birds would have to

lie on their backs and scratch to keep from being covered up. "[81]

It is certainly to be expected that the disastrous and infamous Blizzard of '88 found a place in the tall-tale repertoire:

"The storm came up suddenly one afternoon. I was busy in front of the store, removing from the sidewalk a display of kippered herring, horse collars, buggy whips, rubber boots, gallon jugs, and brooms, when I was caught between two snowflakes weighing as much as I did. Of course, I was just a little shaver then. I managed to free myself and hurry home before the storm was too furious. As my sister and I looked out the window we saw neighbors mired in drifts. We had the hired man hurry to the woodshed to get some cobs and we never saw that guy again until the middle of June. Another man who had been doing some repairing around the porch started to climb a drift on the back steps and when he reached the top he was on the roof of the house. Well, we got him safely down to the attic through a trap door.

"In the town hall, operated by Sam Holiday, an 'Uncle Tom's Cabin' troupe was staging a matinee, when suddenly the storm blew many of the spectators and the entire cast out of the building. Ten days later the town marshal and others found Simon Legree, Eliza, and two of the bloodhounds frozen in the ice near Jones Mill at Bow Valley, while Marks the lawyer turned up in July behind a brewery in St. Helena [Nebraska], fifteen miles away. We learned that a traveling man who had a team of horses and a sleigh drove directly into a room on the sixth floor of a hotel in in Omaha.

"Really, Arthur, there was more wind on that day than you'll observe in the campaign waged this fall by Dewey, Truman, Wallace, and the candidates nominated by Dixiecrats. Only a few homes in Hartington had the same roofs after that blizzard. The one that landed on our house came from a farm eighteen miles northwest of the town. Another odd freak—there wasn't a pane of glass left in a home in our community. However, nobody cared, because the ice froze in the window frames and stayed there until the Fourth of July.

"Yes, Arthur, that was some storm."[82]

And the rain too:

"I remember a hard rain we had one time when the water was so deep that we had to send an old gander up to oil the windmill that stood on a hill behind the house."[83]

Dark, threatening storms still rage across the Plains and cause their share of modern problems. A central Nebraska resident recently told me that a thunderstorm so darkened the sky that they had to light candles to see their TV set.

Although tall tale tellers took special pride in the particularly severe conditions of their own home regions, they were known to give credit to the depredations of weather in other Plains states:

"My grandfather has lived in Kansas for forty years and in spite of what you say, I know that it does rain down there and rains hard too. One time they had a small rain in Kansas and the water rose quite fast. A squirrel climbed a tree to keep from drowning, but as fast as he could climb, his tail was in the water all the time until he reached the top of the tree. Then the rain suddenly stopped and the hot sun came out. After this rapid climb, the squirrel was thirsty, but before he could reach the ground the water had all dried up and the poor squirrel nearly choked from thirst."[84]

The editors of the *Nebraska Farmer* commented in regard to that story: "That must have been as hard a rain as fell in Howard County one time. A barrel was lying in the yard with both heads out and the bunghole up, and it rained in that bunghole so hard that it couldn't run out of both ends fast enough and it bursted the barrel."

Without question, hail was the most feared and most talked about form of precipitation. The most common of all Plains hail stories is this one, told by an informant from the Arlington, Nebraska area:

"This hired man had gone to town in a spring wagon. On his return he saw a cloud which became worse and he felt there was hail in the cloud. He tells that when he got home, the back of the spring wagon was filled with hail and not one stone had touched him."[85]

In another version of the same story, a farmer got home dry but his dog, following behind the wagon, had to swim the whole way.[86]

A similar story appears in my *Treasury of Nebraska Pioneer Folklore*, except that in that case the driver was racing a rainstorm and though he arrived home bone-dry his new prize dachshund that had been riding in the back of the wagon was drowned.[87] And in a Kansas version a load of chickens drowned behind a dry driver.[88]

"A fellow who grew up south of Juniata [Nebraska] told me about a hailstorm. When it was over, the hail was as deep as a windmill tower on their place. He said it took all summer to melt and the well was froze solid down to the water."[89]

Of course Mari Sandoz can be expected to produce some feature of folklore about so vital a thing in the Sandhills as moisture:

"Rain makers arose. In eastern Nebraska a Pawnee Indian promised a shower for ten dollars, a soaking rain for twenty. Someone gave him a jug of whiskey and the hail pounded the grain into the ground. It was a good story, told not without envy."[90]

Fog is not a common weather form on the Plains, but it makes up in density what it lacks in frequency:

"A few hardy men were called by a neighbor to help with the shingling of a barn. The morning air was dense with fog. The work progressed nicely; noon came and, after a hearty meal, the workmen went out to resume their work only to find the sky clear and their shingles laid several feet beyond the ridge pole of the barn."[91]

For some, at least, there was escape. Surveyors once found an error in the placement of the Nebraska-Kansas state boundary. They hated to face a certain Nebraska farmer, because they had to tell him that his farm was not in Nebraska, with its tax advantages, but rather in Kansas. They were surprised, however, to see him smile when he learned the news. He certainly was not pleased about the new tax situation, but he was delighted, he said, that he would not have to face any more of those fierce Nebraska winters.[92]

SKI NEBRASKA

FABULOUS LAND

2

There's not a log to make a seat, along the
river Platte,
So when you eat, you've got to stand, or sit
down square and flat;
It's fun to cook with buffalo wood, take some
that's newly born,
If I knew once what I know now, I'd gone
around the horn.
Traditional Oregon Trail song

I have been a stranger in a strange land.
Exodus 2:22

These are the gardens of the Desert, these
The unshorn fields, boundless and beautiful,
For which the speech of England has no name—
William Cullen Bryant

It is hard to guess what the followers of the Oregon Trail
expected as they neared the Plains. On one hand they had
the deliberately deceptive descriptions from companies seek-
ing passengers and from speculators looking for suckers to
buy lots in their paper cities. They all knew that what they
were about to cross was called "The Great American Desert"
and yet they sang of their ultimate goal:

Ho! for Californ-i-a,
As the gold is thar, most everywhar,
They dip it out with an iron bar,
And where it's thick, with a spade or pick
We can dig out hunks as big as a brick.

As we explore the distant shore,
Filling our pockets with the shining ore,
How it will sound as the shout goes round,
Filling our pockets with dozens of pounds.

The lure overcame the lore and by the thousands they came to cross the Plains and then settle there. In *Vanguards of the Frontier*, Everett Dick reports that one roadside dweller found it hard to believe that there could be any people left in the States, so many Crossers had passed his cabin.[1]

Some found the hell they feared and others the heaven they sought. Rufus Sage quoted a colleague who described the glories of the Plains: "I could die here. . .certain of being not far from heaven."[2]

Some viewed the desolation and treelessness of the Plains as a horror, but farmers who had fought, grubbed, and burned stumps and rooted and hauled stones from the ground in the East saw quite a different thing:

" An old friend came from the East to see me, and when he returned, he told everybody for months, 'Greatest country! Why John took me in a buggy over a hundred miles and the wheels never struck a stone and you can plow a mile without turning around. Think of that!' Of no future state, just as it lies out doors, without artificial aid will it again be said, 'Tickle the land with a hoe and the crop laughs to the harvest.' "[3]

Even cowboys who disdained any attachment with the land felt compelled to comment on its vitality, as this verse from the folksong "The Texas Cowboy" illustrates:

I've worked down in Nebraska
Where the grass grows ten feet high,
And the cattle are such rustlers
That they seldom ever die.[4]

Others thought only of their destinations and saw the Plains only as a broad-gauge obstacle. At one time, it is said, travellers tried to get a resolution through Congress to redefine Nebraska's boundary lines so that the state would run lengthwise north and south instead of east and west—so that it wouldn't take them so long to get across it.

Captain Eugene Ware gives an early—and probably commonplace—evaluation of the western Plains:

"Any private citizen could then, if he wanted, come and settle where he pleased, could fence up all the land he pleased, take everything which he saw in sight, and be a king, providing some wild beast or wild Indian or wild white man did not seek to kill him, which they probably would in short order. But these hostile forces were nowhere to be seen. I asked General Mitchell what he would give for ten miles square amid that beautiful scenery, and he said, 'All I could do would be to look at it. I have now looked at it. I would not give a dollar for a hundred square miles of it. It is of no use to anybody but animals and Indians, and no white man can live here unless he becomes both an animal and an Indian.'

"There was no help from concurring in his views as we looked over the scenery. It was good for nothing but to look at. None of us ever dreamed that it could ever be cultivated or settled up, or become the home of white people, and made up into townships and counties and organized society. The very idea would have seemed preposterous. We were from humid lands, and here everything was a beautiful desert."[5]

Today we are used to the great distances of the Plains and speedy transportation reduces the miles to seconds, but still today Europeans go slack-jawed at the sheer bulk of the Plains. Imagine what goes through the mind of the German, from whose village three or four other villages can be seen, when he travels in Nebraska from Bartlett to O'Neill (42 miles), Burwell to Atkinson (57 miles), or Thedford to Valentine (65 miles), without seeing one town—or for that matter much of anything else but grass. Once I drove from Grand Island to Pine Ridge, South Dakota, with assorted excursions into the interior of the Sandhills, with a young man from

England. I almost feared that he would burn out from his wonder at the immensity of it all.

On another occasion, Earl Dyer of the *Lincoln Star* and I were driving back from Pine Ridge to Lincoln when we met a car coming from the other direction; there was something peculiar about the car—both of us felt it and mentioned it but neither of us could pin down the unusual factor about it, until Earl figured out that the reason it seemed so strange was that it was the first car we had encountered that morning after over two hours of driving.

The thin population must have been especially unsettling for pioneers from Europe. Four Nebraska counties (Arthur, Cherry, Grant, and Hooker) have never reached a population density of two persons per square mile; others (Thomas, Blaine, McPherson, Garden, Morrill, and Kimball) reached two per square mile at some point but have since fallen back below that level.[6] A storyteller once told me that ". . .neighbors were so far apart in pioneer Nebraska that everyone had to have their own tomcat."[7]

A narrator in *Kansas Folklore* recalls that farms were so large that when he set out to plow a field he had a boy planting corn behind him and when he finally reached the end of the furrow and turned around, he found that the corn had already grown up and was ripe, so he just husked his way home, arriving there just in time to celebrate New Year's Eve.[8]

HILLS

The Plains are hardly noted for their hills and mountains, but what there are of them are worthy of comment, as even the earliest Plains Crossers noted. Chimney Rock, Scotts Bluff, and Windlass Hill are repeatedly mentioned in pioneer accounts, as Merrill Mattes notes in *The Great Platte River Road*. He reports one account, for example, that the Chimney Rock had grown out of a stone thrown at a jack rabbit by the legendary mountaineer Jim Bridger.[9]

Chimney Rock would most certainly have drawn attention if it were standing anywhere else, but located as it is after what must have seemed like endless miles of flat and uninteresting prairie, it seized the traveller's attention with a particularly firm grip and held it for the days it took to pass out of sight of the impressive pinnacle.

The clear western air, which still surprises me today, engendered some peculiar ideas about Plains landmarks. Dr. T., in his diary of Oregon Trail travels, describes a foot expedition launched one day during a rest period by some hardy adventurers who wished to see the Chimney Rock at a closer angle. They guessed that they could reach it after a brisk hike of about two miles, only to find after trudging for *seven* miles that it was, according to some, no closer than when they left the wagons several hours earlier![10]   Those baffled fellows must surely have thought that they had been transported to Alice's Wonderland, where the Queen could say, "Now, *here*, you see, it takes all the running you can do, to keep in the same place.   If you want to get somewhere else, you must run at least twice as fast as that!"

There were frequent reports that the Chimney Rock had been substantially taller in the not too distant past and there were abundant explanations for its truncation.   One old mountaineer said that when he first saw the Rock about 1818, it was a good deal taller than then, 1848.   But, he said, it had been struck by lightning during a very bad electrical storm and "knocked off about two miles."[11] I am not sure whether that means that two miles were knocked off of the Chimney or whether the top was thrown two miles, but in either case the story is mighty tall.

And again one must wonder with Alice that things get "curiouser and curiouser":

"Some years ago lightning is supposed to have struck

this hill, whereby about one-half of it was dissevered. The Indians and mountaineers who beheld this catastrophe aver that masses of rock and earth were hurled to the distance of two or three miles. . .and the remarks here of the Indians and others who saw this event may not be uninteresting. One declared half the hills were swallowed up; another, that the rocks were bent in two; but the most ridiculous opinion is one from the Indians, who positiviely [sic] asserted that the rock grew to such a height above the surface of the prairie that the moon once came in the shape of a powder horn—caught the top—and broke it asunder in the middle!"[12]

The popular notion frequently has the Plains table-top flat, which is mostly true northward into the Dakotas and the middle Canadian provinces, but in the south, in Nebraska and Kansas, hills roll on ceaselessly, sometimes attaining surprising pitches. Lewis B. Dougherty said of Windlass Hill near Ogallala:

"I cannot say at what angle we descended but it is so great that some go as far to say 'the road hangs a little past the perpendicular!'"[13]

A Nebraskan told me that the place he "grew up in was so hilly you had to look up the chimney to see if the cows were coming home."[14]

Another Nebraskan says the place she came from is *really* hilly:

"They farmed mighty steep hills those days and visitors always asked how they planted corn on those hills. . . [One] of the answers the natives gave them [was that] they loaded shotguns with corn and fired them into the air over the hills.[15]

"They held the cultivator in the ground on one side to keep it from falling off the hill." ("This is partially true," the informant added.)[16]

H. G. McClintock of Pawnee County, which lies in the southeastern part of Nebraska, claimed that it was so hilly in that country that he had "a spring on his place and it is downhill all the way from his house to the spring and all the way back."[17]

John Daniels, from Dawes County in the hilly northwestern part of Nebraska, said that "in his attempt to build a road through his farm [and] miss the hills he got the road so crooked that he has to muzzle his lead team when hauling hay to keep them from eating all the hay off the rack as they go around the turns."[18]

The *Farmer* discussed the Nebraska hill problem by publishing the following tale submitted by Arthur Nelson of Custer County, which lies in the hilly central part of the state:

"Two of Nelson's neighbors who lived on the opposite slopes of a steep hill had a quarrel. They could not settle the argument in words and so one of them clinched the other's radishes by tieing [sic] knots in the roots on the opposite side of the hill. Mr. Nelson said that he plants his potatoes so that the rows run up and down hill. In the fall he simply opens up the bottom hill and the whole row runs out."[19]

Finally, it was reported from Boone County, in the hilly northeastern part of Nebraska, that "the farmers have to tie their cows together, one on each side of a hill, to keep them from falling out of the pasture." Mrs. Farmenski puts breeching on her hens so they can back the egg into the nest and the hogs use their ears for rough locks in going down hill.[20]

It is clear that the hills were extraordinary, like everything else, but the pioneers seemed capable of adapting to them. I cannot imagine, however, even the best of those hardy champions managing to get used to hills like those described by Bud Nelson of Boyd County in Nebraska's hilly northern reaches:

"Mr. Nelson said that a sand hill kept forming ahead of his team as he drove home from town and his team had a steep uphill pull the entire twelve miles home."[21]

MUD

Just as the dust storm was the natural extension of the wind and drought, the logical progression from excessive rain and dust is mud, and just as you might expect, Plains mud offered its own special kinds of problems.

I should have known better. I have spent enough time in Nebraska and put in enough miles on farm lanes and country roads, but once when I was winding my way back into the Sandhills north of Stapleton, Nebraska, in search of a house built of baled hay, I came upon a great spread of water—perhaps thirty feet across—on the ruts I was calling a road at the time. I knew that Sandhills lakes are rather shallow affairs and I was not at all anxious to try to push my low-slung car out of the ruts onto the uncertain surface around the puddle-pond. As I sat there picking up my courage to drive through, I saw a four-wheel drive pickup truck bouncing toward me across the blow-outs and yucca. The driver, a grizzled veteran of the Sandhills, stopped and rolled down his window, presumably on the assumption that anyone on this road was certain to be having trouble of some kind, be lost, or mad, or all of the above. I asked about the house and he assured me that I was on the right route. Then I asked him if he thought I might drive through the water. "If you're through with your car," he replied.

Apparently my experience was only a latter-day repeat of another, pioneer event:

"We lived at Elk Creek, Nebraska, on the Nemaha River bottom. In the winter we would get almost two feet of frost on the ground. When it would thaw out, farmers would have to have four horses on a front end of a wagon to get to town. One time a fellow was walking across the river road when he seen a hat laying in the road, so he gave it a kick and it was on a man's head. He asked him if he needed help and he said, 'I guess not; I'm on horseback.'"[22]

That particular story is a very common one in American

folklore, so I was especially happy to receive this one, which explains from the unfortunate's point of view how a thing like this might happen:

"One day I was out riding my horse on the banks of the Loup River. I had to cross the river to check on the cattle and upon doing so, I (and the horse) sunk down so deep that all I could see was the blue sky through the opening of the hole above me. The horse died, of course, so I sat there on it for days, not able to move. My horse began to decay, and as it decayed it began to smell. This attracted some buzzards which began to swoop down around the hole's opening above me. As one buzzard swooped close, I grabbed its legs and it pulled me right out of the hole! I hung on for dear life, but I could hang on only so long and finally had to let go. I fell into more quicksand but this time the quicksand was only waist-deep. And you know, I had to walk a whole mile to get a shovel to dig myself out."[23]

The railroads had their share of trouble (and caused more than their share) in crossing the Plains, what with Indians, buffalo, ravines, and broad rivers lying in the path of the iron road. Weather and mud that so plagued the farmer also got into the way of the laying of rails:

"When the old F.E.&M.V. built up through this country the grading gang was certainly up against a proposition. The surveyors had laid out the right-of-way right across the swamps at the head of the Elkhorn. The land was too wet to work at all—horses and oxen mired down and, of course, in those days there were no caterpillar tractors. Why, it was so muddy that the ducks and geese would bog down as they tried to fly over it.

"So what did they do? They first built a fence similar to a snow fence and then sat down there and waited until they got one of those old sou'westers from down Kansas way. The air was full of dust for about four days and when it quieted down there was as good a grade in back of that old fence as anyone could wish for. And that's the truth!"[24]

Ray Harpham of Holstein, Nebraska, seems to have a story for just about everything else and he did not disappoint me when it came to mud:

"And mud! I started for school, but every step forward I took, I slid two backward. I solved that one by turning around and starting home." [25]

The sod houses of the pioneer years on the Plains were well suited to the cold and heat, the wind and prairie fires, but most ·had their weaknesses in the roof. When it rained outside, it rained inside; and when it had stopped outside, it generally continued to drip inside the house for another couple of days. Pioneer wives recall having to cook while holding an umbrella over the soup and arranging pots and pans to keep the drips from turning the tamped-earth floor into a muddy swamp. Sometimes the deep window wells would be the only dry spots in the whole home. And the mire caused its share of problems with the animals too:

"All the hogs in a certain locality were dying of a strange disease. The owners were solely distressed; they couldn't fathom the mystery.

"Finally a young county agent was summoned. After spending several weeks in the vicinity diagnosing and analyzing the case he made the startling discovery that they died of starvation. The yokels were at a loss to account for that as they had all been heavy feeders. He proved his assertion however. He told them that the hog lots had become so muddy through recent rains that large gobs of mud had accumulated on the tails of the hogs, which grew heavier every day. This increasing weight had a tendency to stretch the skin backward as the hogs moved about, and finally had become so bad that the eyes were forced shut, and the animals had starved to death because they couldn't see to eat.

"The farmers decided that the young county agent was the frog's chin whiskers, but when they went to present him with suitable reward they found that he had succumbed to brain fever in trying to think of a word of three letters that means an animal which begins with 'h' and ends with 'g'." [26]

Obviously, the farmers were grateful to the young man for his ingenious analysis but unfortunately his genius was not meant to shine and bring light on other dark areas of Plains agriculture.

The western reaches of the Plains are rarely troubled with mud. The sandy soil does not lend itself well to mudballs. As one settler observed, "One man's land is another man's sand—in Nebraska." And even where the soil might be coaxed into an occasional mudball, there just isn't enough rain. And one man's curse is another man's blessing:

"Many of the early settlers of Nebraska came from the Ohio Valley. A number of years ago I met one of these pioneers who had taken a homestead in the Sandhills. He had come from the lowlands of Illinois and was complaining about the hot winds, the drought, and drifting sand. He said, 'Why, back in Illinoy where I come from we used to cuss the mud. If you walked around in it your feet would accumulate so much of it that you had to kick it off; and you had to be danged careful too when you threw your leg out to let the mud fly off or you would unjoint yourself at the hip and be crippled for life. That's the greatest satis-faction I get a-living here—your feet don't get muddy. And if I get a corn crop I can raise hawgs without having to keep cracking the mudballs off of their tails. Why, back where I come from I lost a hundred shoats one year; the mudballs on their tails kept getting bigger and bigger until they pulled the skin on them shoats so far back that they couldn't shut their eyes and they died for want of sleep. It's easy to farm and raise hawgs here, Mister—if I get a crop. Yessir, the cultivator scours better, the hawgs don't have mudballs, and the children can walk two miles to school right after a heavy rain without me and mamma having to worry about any of them getting a leg disjointed. I sure do like it here—when it rains.'"27

RIVERS

At first glance it may seem strange logic to order a chapter section "Rivers"right after one on "Mud, "but one need only read a few pioneer accounts of Nebraska rivers before one sees that the truly logical thing to do would be to include both under the same heading. Most Easterners even today insist that all Plains rivers should correctly be called creeks and all Plains creeks should go unmentioned.

Of the Missouri River, Everett Dick notes, "The Missouri River honestly merited its nickname 'Old Muddy,' because, according to Horace Greeley, it was so muddy that an egg dropped in a glass of its water became invisible." Senator Thomas Hart Benton facetiously described it as "a little too thick to swim in and not quite thick enough to walk on."28 A variation on the same theme was the popular comment that the Missouri was "too thick to drink and too thin to plow."

Mark Twain had a special affection for rivers in light of his piloting days, and his comments about the Missouri suggest that Professor Dick might have been a bit quick with his adverb "facetiously" in the above passage:

"We were six days going from St. Louis to 'St. Jo'—a trip that was so dull, and sleepy, and eventless that it has left no more impression on my memory than if its duration had been six minutes instead of that many days. No record is left in my mind, now, concerning it, but a confused jumble of savage-looking snags, which we deliberately walked over with one wheel or the other; and of reefs which we butted and butted, and then retired from and climbed over in some softer place; and of sandbars which we roosted on occasionally, and rested, and then got out our crutches and sparred over. In fact, the boat might almost as well have gone to St. Jo by land, for she was walking most of the time anyhow."[29]

Twain crossed Nebraska on his way to Nevada, as described in his *Roughing It*. He saw the most notable feature of the territory, the Platte River, and with his sense of humor, was compelled to comment on so singular a body of "water":

"The Platte was 'up,' they said—which made me wish I could see it when it was down, if it could look any sicker and sorrier. They say it was a dangerous stream to cross now, because its quicksands were liable to swallow up horse, coach, and passengers if an attempt was made to ford it. But the mails had to go, and we made the attempt,"[30] and succeeded despite a few hesitations and bumps which must have given the passengers some cause to wonder about the certainty of their futures.

D. A. Shaw, in his *Eldorado, or California As Seen by a Pioneer*, wrote a typical assessment of the Platte:

It is "useable only if filtered and strained with a cloth since this is not a river at all, but 'simply moving sand.'"[31]

Early settlers told of catching Platte River catfish wearing goggles—to keep the sand out of their eyes.[32]

There was a good deal of talk about underground rivers and lakes—perhaps on the assumption that since there were none on top of the ground there must be some below. The naturally saline ground waters under Lincoln gave rise to the belief that an ocean lay beneath the capital city.[33]

But eventually it became clear that the parched sod was only a reflection of what lay below. A settler continued to walk one-half mile every day to get his day's supply of water from a neighbor's cistern. When asked why he did not just drill his own well, he replied that he was afraid it might be just as far one way to water as the other.

An Omaha informant told me the sad story of his father, who spent almost his last cent trying to locate a well on his homestead. Finally, on what had to be his last attempt, he hit a booming supply of water—only to find that it tested out at only 10% moisture content.[34]

TREES

This is certain to be a short section: there were none. Early travellers are constantly expressing their amazement at finding that even along the major rivers, where one *always* finds trees, on the Plains there were none, just plum brush and willow thickets. A few highland ravines held clumps of gnarled cedars, and the few tall cottonwoods along the trail were rare enough to serve as distinct landmarks, and some even had names. Mari Sandoz calls her readers' attention to this feature of Plains geography in her subtle way when she describes the suicide of a pioneer woman:

"She had plodded the five miles to the Stone cottonwoods for a tree big enough to hang herself."[35]

As a result of my studies of Nebraska history and folklore, I was aware of the stunning absence of trees in 19th century Nebraska, but the matter was brought to me most graphically one time when I was talking with a young student from Potter, Nebraska, a small town on the desolate stretch between Kimball and Sidney in the Nebraska panhandle. I asked her how she was adjusting to school life in Lincoln. She said it took sometime to get used to city life, because for her it had always been a big thing just to go to Kimball on a shopping trip, but she was, she felt, making the adjustment. Except for one thing that she simply would never get used to. I asked her whatever that could be. With a very sincere uneasiness in her eyes and voice, she explained that she had lived in Potter for her seventeen years without ever being hit on the head by a tree leaf, but now, constantly, everywhere it seemed, she was being bombarded by leaves. "It just drives me crazy," she concluded, shaking her head.

(As I write that story, I also recall another coed from a small town who, when I explained to a grumbling class that a vacation assignment "would keep them off the streets," corrected me, "street.")

TOWNS

Predictably, another short section. Several years ago I received a telephone call from a helpful Nebraskan who was guiding me to a house made of railroad ties in Authur, Nebraska. "Where is Arthur?" I asked.

"In Arthur County," he replied.

"Where in Arthur County?" I asked, trying to pin down the site more precisely.

There was a confused moment of silence and then the caller said, obviously being tolerant of my ignorance, "Arthur is the only town *in* Arthur County."

I suspect that the citizens of Bucktail, also in Arthur County, might have objected to the statement, should either one read it, but since then I have noted that there are several counties in Nebraska comprising a substantial area in which there is only one town of any size: for example, Mullen in Hooker County, Oshkosh in Garden County, Harrisburg in Banner County, and Harrison in Sioux County.

But in pioneer days the situation was even worse (or better), as speculators and promoters designed soaring, bustling cities and sold lots to eager-but-innocent buyers, who on their arrival found that absolutely nothing existed of the city except perhaps the lot markers. Many "cities" consisted of nothing more than stakes in the ground, perhaps only *a* stake in the ground.[36]

When the building boom began, however, it seemed that

it might just take over. Colonel Barnabas Bates is said to have introduced a bill into the Nebraska Territorial Council to reserve every eighteenth section of land for farming purposes, since the madness for laying out townsites was spreading so widely. "It has been said that a steamboat captain was a fool to haul passengers when he could have made a fortune freighting town stakes."[37]

Not all of the cities were even as substantial as surveyors' stakes either. Prairie dogs that had been taking care to see that a settler did not make much progress with his farming by digging up crops saw a mirage city on one hot Nebraska day and were so amazed by the incredible progress that they all fell over and died of mortification. "Most of them did anyway," the tale concludes.[38]

The *Nebraska State Journal*, July 5, 1887, carried a story concerning just how serious the problem had become:

"Nothing causes the Nebraska farmer more dismay than to return from town after spending a few hours there and find that his farm has been converted into a thriving city with street cars and electric lights during his absence. But such things will occur now and then and should be regarded with comparative calmness."[39]

FERTILITY

That last story can serve as an introduction to another type of lie that came to enjoy popularity on the pioneer Plains: the unblushing, flagrant, indisputable boast. As I have mentioned before, everything occurred in precise opposites: when it was not hot, it was brutally cold, and when it was not bone-dry, it was flooding, and finally, when it was not a matter of incredible hardship, it was a time of boundless prosperity.

A song based on "Beulah Land," sung variously in these

parts as "Sweet Nebraska Land," "Sweet Dakota Land," "Sweet Kansas Land," and "Sweet Saskatchewan," catalogs some of the miseries of homesteading and concludes with the couplet:

> We do not live; we only stay,
> 'Cause we're too poor to move away.

But the song also had a counterpart, a song sung to the same tune, that celebrated the abundance and joys of Plains life:

> I've reached the land of sun and rain
> Out of Nebraska's verdant plain,
> Where everything grows so fast,
> It takes your breath as you go past.

Another verse asserts:
> The wheat and oats are ten feet tall,

And yet another:
> Our pumpkins are large and round,
> Our sugar beets weigh twenty pound.

The song boasts on:
> Our corn it is so very big,
> One ear will fatten a Berkshire pig,
> Our chickens crow both night and day.[40]

Pioneer memories appear to support the claims set to verse in that song:

"The soil on our place was especially fertile. A footprint in damp soil would grow overnight to three feet long. We had to carry a ten-foot step ladder set up in the wagon at corn-picking time to reach up to pick the ears."[41]

The situation was even more dramatic in Kansas, where —if you can believe everything you hear—it was said that just dipping one's foot in Kansas mud could cause it to sprout roots and grow so big that it was necessary to wear *at least* size 18 shoes. And an unfortunate boy who climbed a cornstalk was unable to get down because the stalk grew a good deal faster than he could slide down.[42]

It must have been just that kind of cornstalk that old-timers say had to be husked from ladders, the ears being cut off by two men with a cross-cut saw. (In case you are interested, the ears were hauled to the crib by four horses—a full team to each ear—while the stalks were shipped east to be used for telephone poles or to be sawed off in short lengths to serve as car wheels.)[43]

On still, hot, July nights I have stood in the fields and "listened to the corn growing." That sounds like the grossest kind of imagination, until you think about those ten- and twelve-foot cornstalks on display at county and state fairs. In 1968 Lincoln's radio station KFOR sponsored a corn-growing contest—with the winner, Rita Overton of Lincoln, submitting a stalk twenty-two feet high, which grew in her backyard flower garden.

So perhaps the following story is not so tall after all:

"Mr. [M. E.] Nelson said that the soil is so fertile [near Howe, Nebraska] that they have to spread a blanket on the ground to feed their chickens on to keep the corn from sprouting before it can be eaten. Mr. Nelson said they planted some corn one afternoon and the next morning it was up. He grabbed an ear and before he could let go it had lifted him so high above the ground he was afraid to let go. His father tried to chop the stalk down but it grew so fast he couldn't hit twice in the same place and if it hadn't been for Claude McKelvie's bull that came to the rescue he would never have got down."[44]

Mrs. Edward H. Duering of Bloomington, Nebraska won a copy of Tom Masson's *Annual for 1924* for this contribution to the *Nebraska Farmer*'s contest:

"A Nebraskan and a Californian were boasting one day of their respective states. The Californian was advertising as usual, and finally the gentleman from Franklin County could stand no more. 'Fertile soil,' he snorted. 'Say, you don't know what fertile soil is. When I was homesteading in Nebraska we lived in a one-room sod house with a dirt floor. We had twin babies and one of them had to sleep on the floor, and every morning I had to get my scythe and mow the grass in the house before we could find the baby.

"'And grow! Why, that baby grew so fast, sleeping on that fertile soil that he was a man, grown and with children of his own, before the other twin was out of long clothes!'"[45]

The editors accepted that story without much fuss, and added:

"The soil seems to be quite fertile universally all over Nebraska. We have been told of ground so rich that it is necessary to mount the watermelons on sleds to keep them from being worn out by being dragged about the field by the rapidly growing vines."

Apparently some of Nebraska's fertility washed or blew over into neighboring states too—Colorado and Kansas, for example:

"When we moved out here to this part of Colorado, it was in the spring of the year, and we needed some potatoes. I sent one of the boys over to a neighbor who, I had heard, had raised some pretty big ones. I told the boy to get one hundred pounds. The neighbor told the boy to go back and tell his dad that he wouldn't cut a potato for anybody."[46]

Indeed, the prosperity of the land brought Stanley Harris of Miller to wax eloquent and poetic:

> I bought a farm in '20
> (Third down, and cheap as dirt)
> Just when the war was over
> And things were on the spurt.
>
> The crops turned out prodigious,
> With prices on the kite.
> We paid the mortgage promptly,
> And fixed the place up right.
>
> We keep a corps of servants,

To whom we pass the buck;
They keep things running smoothly
For just their bed and chuck.

With corn and hay and punkins
We've beat the catalogs;
No pip molests our chickens,
No flu among our hogs.

The calves appear in trios;
We need no cattle loans.
I fed five hundred yearlings,
And I made ten thousand bones.

I bought a gob of "long shot" stock,
Ten cents a throw (preferred).
She rose in value far above
Their sacred, written word.

I've sent the kids to college,
And bought the wife a yacht.
While I just roll in luxury
And count the jack I've got.

There just may have been a few farmers struggling to prove a homestead on the arid, sandy Kinkaid claims who could not laugh very heartily at that one.

The Plains were the best of the States, and each state was the best of the Plains, and each county, it seems, was the best of the state:

"Out here in York County, when you talk about there being a better county in the state, every beet gets red in the face, every potato winks its eye, every onion grows stronger, every oat field is shocked, the rye strokes its beard, the corn pricks up its ears, and every foot of ground kicks. There is no better county than York in the whole state!"[48]

Sunflowers apparently flourished in Kansas soil much the same as corn. There are instances where they were cut up for firewood (not altogether a tall tale) and others found service as railroad ties. Another farmer, who built a barn out of sunflower-stalk logs, made the mistake of tying his cow to a growing stalk to keep her from wandering, only to find the next morning that the stalk had grown during the night, carrying the cow forty feet into the air by her halter.[49]

The longest, most complex, and best sustained Plains lie I have encountered is "Skunk Oil's Pumpkin," collected in the thirties under the W.P.A. by the Federal Writers' Project and reprinted in 1966 in my *Treasury of Nebraska Pioneer Folklore.* A fellow with the descriptive name of Skunk Oil runs across a few stray pumpkin seeds while planting corn. He sticks them in the ground and then forgets them as he goes on with his work. During the summer he is so concerned with his other chores, including searching for a lost sow and her shoats, that he never gets around to walking that section of his crops. When he finally does go there in the fall, he finds a pumpkin vine of horrendous size, so large in fact that he can drive his wagon on it, using it as a bridge wherever it crosses creeks in its route. He hears a noise in one of the gigantic pumpkins and upon chopping his way into it finds his sow and the shoats, all fat and happy, for they had been living on the pumpkin pulp, sheltered from the weather, and so he left them there for the winter.

The next spring Skunk Oil decided to plant one of the seeds from that huge pumpkin, and so he gets some neighbors to help him load one into a wagon. Unfortunately the slippery seed slides from the wagon bed and breaks one of the neighbor's legs. Everyone then decides that if they let this kind of thing go on, that blasted pumpkin just might take over the whole blamed countryside and cause God knows what kind of trouble. So they just burn up the whole mess.[50]

Kansas too had its share of pumpkin tales, including one about a huge pumpkin that was dragged along the ground by its rampant vine until a hole was rubbed into its side.

Three cows entered the pumpkin and were found by the far-mer only after he heard them mooing inside the orange mon-ster. This farmer did better than his Nebraska neighbor, Skunk Oil, however, for he cured the pumpkin and used it for a wagon shed.[51]

As should be obvious by now, even good things were car-ried to painful and troublesome extremes in this strange land. In fact, some Kansans claimed that they were grateful for the grasshopper plagues that swept over the Plains, for they kept the wheat from running wild and taking over the entire country. They say the kernels on that Kansas wheat were so plump that one kernel when baked would make plenty of bread for a family of seventeen (plus ten servants).[52]

I for one, however, am not completely satisfied that it was the soil that caused such fabulous growth. For example, the following story suggests that it was actually the beneficence of the sun that caused all the strange happenings:

"One morning an early pioneer housewife, Hattie, in her haste to get breakfast on the table for the hungry family, burned the sourdough pancake she was baking. She quickly threw it out the door onto the kitchen step for the birds and beasts to feast on. Just as the pancake landed, the sun rose over the canyon rim and ballooned the pancake into a huge straw stack in the nearby meadow. Hattie's husband, Sam, rushed out to haul in the straw for bedding his hogs. At the edge of the straw stack he saw a family of mice. He lifted a fork full of straw above them and let in more Nebraska sun-shine and fresh air, which ballooned the mice into Herford cattle. Thus he had a nice herd, and was soon getting rich selling cream at Walworth, the first cream station in that area."[53]

BIG MEN

3

There were giants in the earth in those days. . .
mighty men which were of old, men of renown.
Genesis 6:4

Man seems to have an insatiable need to create bigger-than-life heroes, and folklorists seem to have an insatiable need to examine those heroes. It is easy enough to understand that, for these heroes are indeed curious figures. Who has not been struck by the contradictory natures of classical gods, by the human foibles of the Teutonic deities? Why is a common thief like Jesse James elevated to the role of a cultural hero? Who will be the folk heroes of the future, if there will be any at all? (At the time of this writing, I asked several people this question, and they replied most frequently, "The man who first set foot on the moon;" yet only two of them could name that man.)

The situation of the culture hero in America is severely complicated—and thereby made all the more interesting—by commercial and opportunistic exploitation of the hero motif. Some writers have deliberately created folk-like figures for the purpose of fooling the public into believing that the characters are indeed traditional, and these confidence men have been labelled by Richard Dorson, director of Indiana University's Folklore Institute, "fakelorists," and justifiably so. But the epithet has also been unjustly applied to purely commercial efforts that have since been taken over by fakelorists or popular culture media.

Nebraska's Febold Feboldson, the colossal Swede from Gothenburg, is an example of this latter class. Febold was used in a Gothenburg newspaper to sell lumber, and, after all, it is not part of the businessman's task to maintain folklore-tradition integrity in his advertisements! It seems to me that it is to the folklorist's profit that Febold was created and promoted, and became successful, for here we see popular culture reflecting a need of the people. In other words, that Febold was a success tells us that there was a need and acceptance here on the Plains for that kind of hero; that the figure of Febold never entered tradition—that is, never became a part of Plains folklore—is neither good nor bad; it is simply a fact.

Louise Pound, Nebraska's foremost folklorist (and one of the foremost in the country), wrote that the Febold legend was never encountered in oral circulation and that his promotion was primarily commercial and never traditional. That has been my experience in gathering this collection: I have never heard one Febold story told in the field as a part of traditional oral circulation. Miss Pound concluded, "The character Febold, the strong man, and his name seem to have been created by Wayne Carroll, a local lumber dealer, who wrote a column under the name Watt Tell in the now defunct Gothenburg, Nebraska, *Independent*. The series began about 1923. Later Carroll used Febold in advertising that he wrote for his lumber company."[1]

Not only have I never met Febold in my folklore field work, but neither have I found many identical motifs from Febold tales in traditional folklore. Of the approximately 110 tales in the book, *Febold Feboldson: Tall Tales from the Great Plains*,[2] only ten are similar to tales I have collected orally from informants or which have appeared in popular culture publications. But not one of these tales appears associated with the name of Febold; they are told primarily as true tall tales or lies, with localization and personalization.

As is the case with popular culture and Febold Febold-son, it is hard to find historical figures that have made their way into the gallery of folk heroes of the Plains. No doubt this stems from the pioneer farmer's contempt for the usual figures of historical eminence: politicians, generals, and business magnates; and whatever folklore arose about these characters is not fit for the ears of mixed company and certainly was not the stuff of heroes.

The few spokesmen the homesteaders had on their side were so short-lived that they did not allow much time for the development of heroic-legend cycles. Furthermore, the historical realities of some of their leaders would put most legendary exploits and language to shame:

"All the wit and anger of the [Populist] movement seemed to be distilled into the fiery essence dispensed at rallies by dragon-killers (or, as some might prefer, dragons) like Mary Elizabeth Lease, who is supposed to have shouted in Paola, Kansas, words that were to become an immortal slogan: 'The people are at bay. Let the bloodhounds of money who have dogged us thus far beware. What you farmers need is to raise less corn and more hell!' Later she said, 'There are times when I actually made speeches without knowing it, when I was surprised to read in the morning paper that I had spoken the night before. . . .My tongue is loose at both ends and hung on a swivel.'"[3] And it probably was.

It is a common folklore phenomenon that historical figures—perhaps of only local or regional notoriety—assume legendary stature. Sometimes they themselves embroider their reputations; sometimes admirers and friends do the legend weaving; usually both factors elevate the lucky person to the enviable stature of "Legend."

An excellent example of this kind of development is Jim Bridger, the famous and infamous 19th century adventurer, explorer, trader, trapper, and mountain man, who ranged throughout the new territories west of the Mississippi River.

He moved with other living legends like Mike Fink, Hugh Glass, and Kit Carson. He consorted with Federal generals and Indian kings—and princesses.

To be sure, Bridger was a remarkable figure in reality as well as in tall tale. For example, he was once wounded by two Indian arrows, one of which could not be pulled out, and the head remained in his body for some time until he next encountered a doctor who pulled it out. Father DeSmet, an early missionary to the lands beyond the Missouri, asked him how he could carry that arrowhead without terrible infection. Jim replied, "In the mountains meat never spoils."[4]

But almost all of his tall tales center about the fabulous land he was in. In short, the remarkable thing about Bridger was that he was one of the first to be here and tell about it. Indeed, his first tall tales were not at all tall but were factual accounts of geographic features that only seemed beyond reality to his audiences.

Imagine what responses met the earliest accounts of Yellowstone, an area of our earth that is hard to believe even after you have seen it yourself:

"They were entering a land of legend now, for nineteen years earlier a trapper named John Colter . . . had returned from a long solitary trip, spinning yarns about the strange and tortured world at the head of the Yellowstone, a world of fire and brimstone where the Low Regions broke through the earth's surface. Few had believed him, and yet Colter's Hell had become permanently woven into the campfire lore of the West. Few would later believe Jim Bridger or any of his brigade mates; another forty-four years would pass before present-day Yellowstone Park was officially discovered."[5]

It was indeed a fantastic land, and others who visited it frequently decided that to talk about it would only be to convince friends and relatives of the damaging air of the mountains. So, like today's respectable citizen who sees a flying saucer or ghost, they just said that they had had an interesting trip and let it go at that.

But Jim Bridger had already spoken and was committed to the miracles of Colter's Hell. He continued telling about that remarkable landscape: "He had an endless store of [tales]—one percent true [like the one about the obsidian peak], and all true like Two-Ocean Pass, where you could stand on a rock in the middle of a creek and spit tobacco to either side, depending on whether you wanted it to end up in the Atlantic or Pacific. . .[or the] great spouts of steam and water that erupted at intervals, 'Thick as a man's body and high as a flagpole,' "[6]

The truth became increasingly "bent," and shrank to less than one percent. Yellowstone became:

"Bridger country—a never-never land of enchantment with lofty peaks that had been deep holes in the ground when Jim first came to the Rockies, with petrified canyons where Jim's mules broke their teeth trying to graze on petrified grass, where the sun had no warmth because sunlight was petrified, where petrified birds sang petrified songs, where Jim had once escaped the Blackfeet by riding straight off through the air because even the law of gravity was petrified. . . . Or maybe the Easterners would hear of Jim's Eight-Hour-Echo Canyon. Whenever he camped for the night in that region, he shouted, 'Time to get up,' down the vast gorge last thing before he rolled up in his buffalo robes. Worked better than an alarm clock."[7]

Some sources report that Bridger resented those who first doubted his stories about Yellowstone, the Rockies, the Great Salt Lake, and the western weather, but feigned indignation is still a trait of the good tall tale purveyor. For example, the Nebraskan who was asked about a peculiar whistle he was wearing on a string around his neck: "An elephant whistle," he retorted. "It'll scare off elephants, no matter how big, or how many, or how mad, or how comfortable they might be."

"Well, there are no elephants in Nebraska," said his companion, not about to be hornswoggled.

"See!" snorted the triumphant plainsman.

Jim Bridger represents an early manifestation of the tall tale on the Plains, and the effects of his skill have been felt in Plains folklore and literature right on up to our own time.

Mari Sandoz put heroic tales and language in the mouth of one of her characters, Milton, of *The Tom-Walker*. First she gave him thoughts reflecting the tall-tale genre:

"He looked over the lights of the town and the gleaming bend of the Ohio—a sickle a man might lash to a pole for a skyhook to pull down a thunderhead."[8]

Then she put in his mouth the pyrotechnic exclamations of such as Mike Fink and Daniel Boone:

"Igonnies, yet! I'm a swivel-jawed, double-jointed rattler and strike both ways. I went through the yellin' Rebs like a dose of croton oil and I fights gougin' something gostratious!. . .Yeh, I'm a hell roarer fer talk."[9]

From there it was an easy step to make him a teller of tall tales:

[Milton, speaking about his peg-leg:] "Snapped off by a coachwhip snake down in Georgia. . . .Yes, sir-ee, bit clean off. But I gloms it away from him an' beats him to death with it, the on-mannerly rep-tile."[10]

And, "So they drove out into the street, Milton, low-down as a snake in a gully for months now suddenly laughing, loudly promising to bring great things home—a gunny sack full of golden eagles, double eagles, and maybe even a Kansas cyclone, hobbled and housebroke, to drive Lucinda's clumsy sewing machine."[11]

Finally, Mari Sandoz has Milton become a truly folk figure, mirroring a progression that has frequently been recorded in scholarly studies of the development of folk heroes.[12] A newspaper editor, with his sensitive ear for a good story, picks up one about the peg-legged Milton:

"Custer County *Buckshot.* . .THE IRON-LEGGED MAN FROM THE MISSOURI. There was a great man abroad on the North Table last week, with thunder in his voice and an iron leg to ground the lightning, or flash out and rip the daylight from around your head. It is said he can hit a ball so it never comes to earth, and has catbirds slipping through his hair like through a plum thicket and bears roaring in his wiskers. We don't know, but we know he has the gift of Hippocrates in his heart and hand, for he saved three lives in one hour up there last week."[13]

And then the people themselves picked up the stories and began to pass them around: the oral communication that distinguishes folk lore.

"By now [Milton's] name and the exploits of his leg had spread from Kansas to Dakota. It was told that he could bat a rock so high it fell in a shower of meteors 'way over Colorado and set the range afire; could jump the Missouri and back without touching the ground on the far side, and with a little oiling he would surely drive off the eclipse coming the 29th of July."[14]

"But the stories of Iron Leg kept growing until some even blamed him for the cyclone over on the Nemaha, since it was well known that by turning on that pipe he could make a wind that chilled everything around him so the ducks thought it was November and scooted off south, the grass died, and the cricks took to gurgling under ice. Some claimed he could whirl himself clean off the ground and sail through the air like a balloon, sparks from his pipe flying out behind him like a comet in the night."[15]

At first ashamed of the stories about their father, stories they labelled "B.S.," Iron-Leg's children gradually began to take pride in their father's fictional feats, as he became, in the novel, a folk hero.

As the Second World War approached and dominated the national consciousness, Iron Leg became substance for rampant nationalism:

"Then there was a new Iron Leg story for the scrapbook:

brought water to Wyoming, boring a mess of wells over
in the foothills and just letting the water run out over the
sagebrush, with Iowa as his homestate taking her claim
on the water rights to court. And up around the dam they
offered to pass the hat and send him over to clip old Musso
in the mush, maybe turn around fast and blow him and
Hitler and their kit and kaboodle scattering like a whirlwind in a fodder pile. "[16]

Then, like everything else interesting and exciting in
folklore and history, the Old Man became grist for the
commercial mill:

"He was a year 'round tourist attraction at the old mine-
boom hotel, autographing his Iron Leg stories published
in a book. With pictures of Jim Bridger, Kit Carson, and
Pack the mountain cannibal, around him, he told stories
of the ghost on the Devil's Stairway and how Colorado
got her gold and silver—the linings melted out of the devil's
pots and kettles when a Kansas cyclone came busting
through and fanned up the hell fire. He bragged about his
grandson too, with a left that could smash a granite boul-
der, or a New York publicity man. "[17]

And now the admiration was mutual, for Martin too had
become a storyteller, perpetuating the heroic figure of his
father—much, we must note, the way Miss Sandoz preserved
the figure of her father in her writing:

"Visiting GI comic dons hospital garb and makes 'em
laugh. Uses Colonel's sock like magic carpet to transport
imagination. Comes by it naturally. GAR grandfather
made Kansas cyclones." [From fictional newspaper arti-
cle].[18]

Louise Pound treats other fragmentary Plains heroes
like Antoine Barada, a historical figure living from 1807
to 1887 and featured in tales of southeastern Nebraska;
and Moses Stocking, who appears in stories about squash
vines dragging their fruit, boys being lost on fast-growing
cornstalks, and pumpkins being used for farm buildings.

In both cases, however, Mari Sandoz was Dr. Pound's primary and only source and few other versions of tales about these men have been found in oral circulation.[19] I dream of the day when some barfly says to me, "Antoine Barada? Old Fred Jensen can tell Barada stories from spring on through harvest," or when a farmer's wife says of her overalled husband, "Don't get him started on Moses Stocking or we'll be up all night."

Buried in the forgotten files of the field collections of the Nebraska Federal Writers' Project are a few scattered stories about Barada which appear on the surface at least to be genuine, oral tales—true folklore. An entry under the name J. H. Norris, dated August 25, 1936, carries stories documented only as "personal observation." According to this informant, Barada was a half-French, half-Omaha giant, who spent two years as a captive of the Sioux. He could lift clear a weight of 1,800 pounds. In addition to the more common accounts of his driving in river pilings by hand, this account relates his wrestling skills: "Antoine was not only ambidextrous—he was also pedeldextrous, which ability he well demonstrated when he won the match by pinching his opponent with his toes while he slapped him into unconsciousness with one blow of his ear." He must have been quite a wrestler, for he was also known to bear-hug bears to death!

Perhaps the most famous story of his skills is that of his broad jump style: "Antoine, who was always a modest man, waited until all the others had competed [in a jumping contest]. The record thus far stood at a distance of ten feet three and one-half inches. However, this was made by a man who used weights which he threw behind him after he was well clear of the ground and high up in the air in the first part of his leap. Since this was a new mode of jumping, Antoine resolved to profit by this novel method of propulsion. Quickly picking up two boulders of about four hundred pounds each, he stepped to the line swinging one on either side of him. With the third swing he leaped and hurled the stones over into Kansas. Spectators held their breath as they saw him mysteriously disappear in the distance. He had leaped so high and so far that dinner had to be postponed for three hours while he walked back. Even the women did not become angry. Instead of harsh words they gasped: 'What a man!' "

Tales that have developed in the area of Humphrey, Nebraska, about John "Bull" Melcher appear to be legitimate folklore, but, as was the case for Dr. Pound, all of my stories come from one source and I have not been able to find anyone else who knows stories from this cycle. Melcher, I was told, was quite a storyteller himself and, just as Mari Sandoz outlined in the development of her own tall-tale teller and subject, he then became the object of other people's tales.[20]

"It seems John was on the way home from Columbus [25 miles] driving a Model-T Ford. Anyway, going up Jawarski Hill [big in those days], he ran out of gas, so switched the key to magneto and drove the rest of the way home."

That is an example of Melcher's quick wit. This next tale is an example of his physical dexterity:

"He was painting his windmill [a wooden tower]. While climbing to the top, a rung' broke so he rode the ladder down as each rung broke. When he hit the ground he hadn't spilt a drop of paint out of a full gallon pail."

And tall tales that have nothing to do with Melcher's own character have also been attached to him:

"How about the time he had a runaway while cutting grain with a binder. As he lived and farmed a creek bottom, there were lots of big cottonwood trees. Well, the team headed for the creek and the binder cut off the trees and never missed tying a perfect bundle."

Finally, one more example of Melcher's physical prowess:

"Or the time he went to get the cows for milking. They

were on the far side of the creek, so he started across on the ice, when he fell through. Not being able to swim and having floated away from the hole he fell through, in desperation, he thought of an unfrozen spot a quarter mile down the stream. So he walked under the ice to the opening."

Perhaps the next story is not, strictly speaking, a "hero tale" or even a tall tale for that matter, but it is one of my favorites and I will justify its inclusion here as an example of the human qualities of the otherwise superhuman pioneer:

"Upon one occasion Aunt Sarah [Finch] was freeing her mind for Uncle Swain's benefit when he shouted, 'If you don't shut up, I'll go out and freeze myself to death in that snow bank!' Aunt Sarah was too much out of patience to remember former frights that she had received by similar threats, and kept right on laying down the law from her understanding of it.

"With eyes glaring into space, clenched teeth, and set features, like a man who contemplates some terrible deed, looking neither to the right nor to the left, he takes down his overcoat and puts it on, buttoning it up to his chin, walks deliberately out and lies down on the snow bank. These movements are followed by two pairs of curious black eyes belonging to his nephews, John and Bob, who look on with mouths wide open, thinking the old man had gone crazy. After a few minutes the freezing man raises himself up on one elbow, looks around and discovers these two pairs of bright eyes watching him through a chink in the woodshed. He motions the boys to come to him and sends Johnny after the buffalo robe, which he carefully wraps around his body, and again lies down to freeze in comfort. As he lies there he pictures Aunt Sarah inside taking on and weeping her eyes out over his sad fate. Catching another glimpse of the bright eyes, he calls their owners to him and inquires, in a stage whisper, 'Say boys, is the old gal a-cryin'?'

" 'Naw, she's laughin'.'

"'Then, by George, that settles it; I won't freeze.' "[21]

And, as is the constant fate of any tall-tale lover, that story reminds me of two others, one about the cold and another about wives.

One nice sunny morning, in the early days, there was a fellow who started out to check his cattle, which lived in the Sandhills twenty miles away. After driving there about midday, a blizzard started in. So he decided he had better head for home, but after going a short distance his horse stepped in a hole and broke his leg. As he didn't want his horse to lie there and die he took out his gun and shot him. Then he decided to take his knife and remove the intestines so he could crawl in out of the storm. After a while the coyotes gathered around. He then reached out and grabbed two coyotes by the tail and managed to steer them by pulling first on one, then the other. Finally he arrived home. [22]

The second story, from a newspaper of 1900, suggests that wives were just as contrary then as they can be now: "A Milford woman fell in the mill dam and when she was rescued a seven-pound catfish was found entangled in her wire bustle. Her husband wanted to set her again, but she wouldn't consent."[23]

During the W.P.A.'s collection work in Nebraska, several tall tales were gathered regarding "Jud Smith's grandfather" in Swan City, Nebraska. He was a big man who had a quart of whisky for breakfast, and when he went on a real drunk he did away with at least five gallons of whiskey. He could drive in horsehoe nails with his bare fists and once held a house down in the face of a tornado. He bent iron bars over his knees without bothering to heat them, and anyone unfortunate enough to be caught in the path of one of his sneezes was liable to be blown clear across town. Once during a shotputting contest he threw a cannon ball so far that it was never found (but there was some comment about a strange cannon ball found buried on the Capitol grounds in Washington, D.C.).[24]

One Nebraskan wrote me that he had performed some rather heroic feats himself. "This particular day in August I was mowing hay . . . with a team of horses and I heard a terrible roar behind me. I looked back and I saw a tornado coming right at me. I knew it was heading straight for my house. I threw the mower out of gear, and started to the house, but we were picked up by the tornado — team, mower, and all. I knew it was heading straight for my old sod house and my loved ones, but I had the presence of mind to throw my mower in gear, and do you know sumpin' — I cut the tail right off that tornado; and team, mower, and myself landed safely 100 yards from the old sod house, believe it or not."[25]

Dan Franck of Audubon, Iowa was recently telling a fellow worker about his father having to climb up the flag-pole in front of the Fairbury, Nebraska courthouse to re-place an iron eagle that had blown off during a particu-larly windy storm. The friend replied, with a straight face, "That was quite a feat, but you know what? My dad used to shinny up that pole each morning and feed it!"[26]

Some men were thoughtful and considerate to humans too: "This one man's girl had a wooden leg and so he gave her a garter and a box of thumbtacks for Christ-mas."[27]

It took a particularly strong kind of courage to face coolly the dangers that seemed to threaten the homesteader at every corner:

"Ernest Witmer, of Stanton, tells . . . that when he found himself facing a ferocious bear . . . he simply rammed his arm down the bear's throat, grabbed him by the tail and turned him wrong side out. The bear kept right on running, but in the opposite direction, and Mr. Witmer got home safely."[28]

Bears are not run-of-the-mill creatures and it takes a special kind of ingenuity to cope with them. Plainsmen were never at a loss for ingenuity: "One day an old-timer decided to go out into the woods hunting. After hunting for some time to no avail, he turned around to go home when he saw a huge grizzly bear coming towards him at a great speed. Afraid he could not make it up a tree in time, he saw an old empty barrel, which he thankfully crawled into. The old bear, realizing a long winter ahead, sat down on the barrel and proceeded to wait him out. Lucky for him, he spied the old bear's tail sticking through the small hole in the barrel. Quick as a wink he tied a knot in her tail, crawled out, and went happily home. The next spring when he happened to be in the same locality, to his amazement he saw momma bear and her three little cubs, each having a tiny barrel on the end of his tail."[29]

And when the pioneer ventured to other parts of the world, he faced dangers there with the same equanimity, as a story told by Anna Kubicek about her uncle well illustrates:

"This uncle . . . was hunting polar bears in Greenland during a dreadful snow storm. He came face to face with a big polar bear and at the same time discovered that he was out of bullets. Realizing his danger, beads of cold perspiration broke out on his forehead, and the arctic air was so cold that those beads froze into balls of ice. One of these [the] uncle seized and rammed in the gun barrel as [a] bullet. Aiming at the bear's head, he fired, but the heat of the discharge melted the ball of ice and it came out of the barrel a stream of water.

"For a moment her uncle thought all was over, but the frigid air again turned the stream into an icicle and pierced the bear's head just above the right eye. However, the heat in the bear's head melted the icicle and it didn't hurt the bear a bit, except that he died of water on the brain."[30]

Those who believe that virtue is never rewarded will be surprised to learn that the editors of the *Nebraska Farmer* awarded Miss Kubicek a fur-lined fountain pen for the above effort.

While Miss Kubicek's uncle was headed north, another Nebraskan with extraordinary skills, Jack Dempcy, was "taking a swarm of bees down to Texas on the hoof and he used a bee-bird for a bell weather and headed them straight for the Texas line. They were going so fast when they hit Texas that they upset the hive as they went in. The next morning Jack made a noise like a sweet clover patch in full bloom and as they came out the consignee counted them and found that they hadn't lost a single bee."[31]

In my two previous chapters, I emphasized the difficulty sometimes of separating the exaggeration from the truth. That can also be the case with the feats of men themselves. Cowboys have always been noted for their willingness to take on absolutely anything, so the following newspaper article from 1890 just might be a baldfaced truth:

AFTER THE TIME OF DAY

"The cowboy has bucked against many things and not many times has he had to own up whipped, but one instance in which he lost has happened. Last week two of the gen-ius cowboys went into town and for several days kept full of bug juice.

"Starting home the two whose names are Skinner and Marks rode near the railroad tracks for a distance. After riding through that country along the tracks for a distance they described a train and, anxious to learn the time of day, called the driver of the 'iron horse' to stop and tell them. The engineer was too busy at the time to comply with their request and passed on without response. This nettled the rushers of the Plains, and the time of day they determined to have. One of them spurred on his bronco and neared the engine, which was not moving particularly rapidly. A swift throw of the lariat and the smoke stack was encircled. The result was not entirely expected. The train hurried on, the saddle-girths remained firm and the horse performed more feats than a circus acrobat. The cowboy stayed with his horse too, for one foot caught in the stirrup and he grabbed his animal's tail to save his life. His friend, taking in the situation, roped the horse of the would-be train-stopper. With the combined pulling of two animals, the lariat about the smoke stack broke and the wild race which had been going on ended.

"The boys later attempted to get a warrant for the arrest of the engineer, but as no one was hurt the commissioner only advised them to get a stouter rope next time."[32]

Now that I consider a triumph of the spirit over the mind. This story, also dated 1890, is to my mind a *tour de force* of practicality and applied physics:

" 'Shorty' Smith, the boss mule packer, while driving his pack train up a steep hill in the western part of the state, had a very exciting experience last week. Part of the mules were loaded with a Frue concentrator. One of the mules, the largest in the train, was loaded with the long side-sills of the concentrator, one on each side, and when the train had got half way up the hill and on the steepest part of the trail, the mule with the timbers gave a lurch sideways and landed about a hundred feet down the hill, and lodged suspended in the air between two oak trees about fifteen feet from the ground. How to get the mule down was the next problem. But like all great packers 'Shorty' was equal to the emergency. He soon took in the situation, rushed up to one of the mules that had some powder, caps and fuse in its pack, which he soon fixed so as to explode the powder, and placed it in the hollow of one of the trees.

"He touched a match to the fuse and yelled, 'Get out of

the road!' And when the shot went off and the smoke had cleared away, 'Shorty' looked around and saw Old Tom— the mule—with his load all on walking up the hill to the rest of the train and not a scratch on him."[33]

These pioneers were brave and strong and fast and clever and a few other things besides. Who would have guessed, for instance, that at least one early settler had the skill to become such a remarkably accurate artist?

"If I could do what my father did, I would not be a farmer! He studied art in his younger days and I remember three of his paintings in particular. He picked up a piece of wood one time and painted it like marble, and it was so natural it would sink when placed in water.

"One time in the early '90's when it was so hot we could hardly stand to be in the house he sat down and painted a winter landscape. He did not get to finish that picture, however, for it began to grow so cold in the room that the thermometer dropped to zero when placed near the picture.

"His next picture was one of my grandfather. It was so natural that we had to shave him every week, and it was real fun for us kids to shave grandpa."[34]

It must have been the soil or the climate, for the Indians who had occupied the Plains before the white invasion also showed many remarkable traits. One recent arrival in the West had heard about the phenomenal memory of one particular Indian who frequented the town. As the stranger left town on the train, he spotted the Indian and thought he would test the fabled memory. He asked the Indian what he had had for breakfast on the morning of August 12, 1852. The Indian answered without hestitation, "Eggs."

The white man boarded the train mumbling under his breath about the perfidy of fraudulent redskins. "Eggs indeed!" But about twenty years later the same man returned to the town and as he got off the train he saw an Indian standing on the platform. Being civil, he greeted the Indian with the traditional "How!" to which the Indian replied, "Scrambled."[35]

One thing is certain: pioneer youngsters developed more than their share of speed and endurance.

"One very hot day in August I walked down to the lake to fish. When I got there I took off my shoes and put my feet in the cool water to cool them off. When I put my shoes back on I looked up and saw a big bobcat just ready to spring on me. I started to run and that bobcat come after me. Round and round that lake I ran and when I thought I could run no more I ran out on the ice and the cat followed me. It slipped on the ice and broke both hind legs and the race was over. I walked across the lake and went home. That cat had chased me from August to December."[36]

"Bullets were often scarce, so when the boys of the family were sent out for rabbit meat, they just ran them down by foot, trotting alongside and feeling the rabbits so they got only the plump ones."[37]

If, after those stories, you can somehow doubt that pioneers were quick-footed, this last one about their speed is certain to convince even the most stubborn of doubters:

A friend from Juniata said his "father was a driver in the Civil War [and] was going down the road with a load of gun powder. The lightning struck and burned up a bushelbasket full before he could tromp the fire out."[38]

The special skills and luck of those early day plainsmen combined with the fertility and abundance of the land to produce some very special effects. One of the most popular of 19th-century frontier stories is that of The Marvelous Hunt:

"Well, it was just about Thanksgiving Day and we didn't feel we had much to be thankful for. I didn't have any shells for my gun but decided to go into the woods to see what I could find for Thanksgiving dinner.

"I waded into the water to cross a creek and my pants

filled up with fish, so full of fish in fact, that my waistband button popped off. That button headed straight for the limb of a tree on the other side of the creek. It split the limb open just wide enough to catch the toes of five wild turkeys sitting on the limb.

"With my pants full of fish, and the toes of five wild turkeys caught by that limb, we had a fine Thanksgiving dinner."[39]

Lizzie Cox of Brewster, Nebraska submitted the following rhymed version of a similar marvelous hunt:

> I went out a-hunting one cold winter's day,
> The flowers they were blooming,
> And the meadows they were gay.
> I tracked me up a great big buck,
> I tracked him in the snow.
> I tracked him to the riverside
> And under he did go.
>
> I loaded up my pistol and underwater went
> To kill the fattest buck, Sir,
> It was my whole intent.
> When I got under water
> Ten thousand feet or more,
> I shot off my pistols —
> Like cannons they did roar.
>
> When I got out of the water, the deer had almost fled
> Across the hills and plains
> 'Till you could scarcely see their heads.
> So I bent my gun a circle
> And shot around the hill.
> Out of five hundred blackbirds
> Ten thousand I did kill.
>
> After I had gathered my venison and skins
> I took them to my forty-foot barn
> But they wouldn't all go in.
> Now my song is ended;

I won't sing anymore.
If you can sing a bigger lie—
You've had the chance before.[40]

Fragments of another classic hunt tale were submitted to the same contest:

"In the good old days a farmer went out to look over his pasture. In looking around he saw a big buck deer upon a tall hill. 'I'll wait until fall when deer season opens. Then I'll have some deer meat,' [he thought]. When fall came he went back to look for the buck deer. After driving over much prairie, he saw a doe in a grove of trees; looking a little further he saw the buck with the doe's tail in his mouth. The buck was blind so the doe was leading him around. [The farmer had only one bullet but would like to bag both deer. He was at a loss what to do—but only for a moment. He shot the doe,] then reached into his pocket, got his knife, cut the doe's tail off, led the buck over to the wagon by the doe tail. [He nailed the doe's tail to the back of the wagon and drove slowly home, leading the buck along behind. When he got there, he reloaded and bagged the buck too.]"[41]

Another hunting story that is one of my favorites tells us something about the pioneer spirit:

"Two men were setting out on a hunting trip. The one who was supposed to furnish the supplies showed up with a surprisingly small sack. 'What you got in there for grub?' asks the one.

"'I've got four bottles of whiskey and a loaf of bread.'

"'Why, you addle-pated numskull!' exploded the other. 'What kind of planning is that anyway? I knew I should have done the buying myself. What the hell are we going to do with all that bread? !'"[42]

That kind of mistake has to be an exception, however, because it is clear that the Plains atmosphere tended to produce folks a trifle more healthy than was even desired.

Some villages, I have been told, finally had to shoot someone so they could get their community cemetery started.

There is currently a lot of fuss about people living longer
in Nebraska, but according to one of my informants, "It
just seems that way here." A pioneer optimist is said to
have once remarked that this must be the best of all possible worlds, and his pessimistic friend added, "That's exactly what I'm afraid of."

As a Nebraskan I find special significance in the fact
that the one story I have about pioneer "puniness" comes
from a collection of *Kansas* lore:

"Three boys were arguing about who had the smallest
father. 'My father is three feet tall!'

"'That's nothing. *My* father is two feet tall.'

"'My father is in the hospital!'

"'Why?'

"'He fell off a ladder picking strawberries.' "[43]
Perhaps that story is just meant to be a commentary on
the size of Kansas strawberries!

I would like to end this chapter on this same note, just
to show that not all Plains pioneers were always superhuman; they made their share of mistakes too:

"[That] was about as funny as Judge Kilgore is said to
have done in the winter of '80. The Judge packed water
two miles for several weeks through two feet of snow till
someone suggested that snow, when melted, made water."[44]

But when they made mistakes, they were not too proud
to admit them and correct them. One of Martha Dirk's informants tells about a man who swam halfway across the
ocean, decided he couldn't make it, and so swam back.[45]

STRANGE CRITTERS

4

All animals are equal, but some animals are more equal than others.

George Orwell

"There ain't no such animal."

Farmer looking at a camel

Tall tales and lies about the strange creatures that occupied the Plains fall roughly into two categories: phenomenal characteristics of otherwise common and ordinary beasts and wholly fantastic beings. I will warn you beforehand that your imagination is again going to be stretched to its limits, but do not forget—so was the pioneer's when he first encountered the everyday inhabitants of this land. The Czech, freshly arrived in this country and trying to patent a homestead, had never before encountered such things as snakes with baby rattles at one end and death at the other. He had met the European cousins of Plains grasshoppers and mosquitos, but they were apparently from an aristocratic branch, enervated from inbreeding, because they were no match for their Plains counterparts.

Just imagine trying to describe a buffalo, the most common of this area's larger citizens, to someone who had no idea what one looked like. I suppose you would start with a cow, but that is a troublesome start at best, and where could you go from there to give an idea of what that woolly-headed, hump-shouldered, broom-tailed, dainty-footed, squint-eyed, pitch-fork horned brute looked like. And then you could start trying to convey his numbers.

Imagine trying to describe in a latter home to your folks

in Sweden the prairie dog towns and bobcats and skunks and gigantic Missouri River catfish and antelope and the great elk that were common here in those days. It is not so surprising that some of the descriptions became a bit too marvelous and that a few descriptions arose for which there were no such critters!

MONSTERS

In fact, the whole adventure of Plains exploration and immigration had the air of a mystical, magical beast about it. Taking part in the fever of westward movement was called "going to see the elephant." No one is really sure where that figure of speech came from—perhaps from P. T. Barnum's elusive and wonderful pachyderm—but it recurs constantly in pioneer accounts, from folksongs to diaries.[1]

Mattes says, "This creature seldom appeared except on the fringes of danger, and then it was only a fleeting glimpse." He quotes Martho Morgan in her *A Trip Across The Plains* . . .. shortly after a buffalo stampede: "I think I saw the tracks of the big elephant." And James Abbey, who felt "a brush of the elephant's tail," and Niles Searles, who "had a peep at his probascis."[2]

Mari Sandoz' tall tale teller, Iron Leg Milton, had distinct recollections of a flying monster that I have not encountered elsewhere:

"I bet what them Swedes been seein' don't compare to the flyin' serpents we had back in the Nineties—quarter mile long, an' smokin' flame. Feller in Texas drug one down with his lassoo an' chopped it up for his hound-dogs."[3] "Newspapers carried stories of. . .a litter of eight boys born to a woman up in Keyapaha county, and of great lighted monsters flying through the night in the Platte River region, down around the Solomon and over in Indiana, and about a flying serpent that stampeded a night herd in west Texas."[4]

There was one Nebraska sandhills monster that existed outside literary publications, the great Alkali Lake (now Walgren Lake) Monster, that gained such notoriety that it was even reported in the pages of the *London Times* in 1923. This monster (labelled by biological taxonomists *Gigantious Brutervious*) reportedly devoured livestock from ranches neighboring the Lake, near Hay Springs, terrorized the area with his thunder-like roars, and turned the hair of at least one would-be debunker snow-white. There were rumors, later, that a mermaid had been caught in the lake, but the reports would not be substantiated, perhaps out of fear of what a game warden might think of a catch like that.[5]

Whatever the truth of the matter, my favorite treatment of the whole subject of monsters comes again from the pen of Mari Sandoz:

"While [Mary] plucked the birds in the meat house and put the feathers into a paper sack to be burned, Jules hunched over the *Standard* spread on his knee, reading to her, chuckling, hiding his pain. Alkali Lake, near Hay Springs, where the early sky pilots dipped their converts, was inhabited by a sea monster—with a head like an oil barrel, shiny black in the moonlight. Some thought it a survival of the coal age. But Johnny Burrows and other fundamentalists of the Flats knew better. The same devil that scattered the fossil bones over the earth to confound those of little faith could plant a sea monster among the sinners. . . .

"When Andy came in [Jules] asked if he had seen anything of the monster. The little grub-line rider took the jew's-harp from between his leathery lips. 'No, cain't say's I has, but I seen lots of the stuff them fellahs as sees 'im drinks.' "[6]

Another totally mythical creature that has been documented in both Nebraska and Kansas is the Sandhill Dodger (with, to date, no scientific designator). This singular creature had legs shorter on one side than the other—so that he could run easily along the sides of the hills. A relatively common tale about this animal tells about the time a cowboy tried to rope one, thinking that he could eventually corner it when it ran out of hills with the right pitch. The Dodger fooled the roper, however, by swallowing its nose and turning itself completely inside out; it then headed in the opposite direction, its short legs still next to the up-slope of the hill![7]

LIVESTOCK

Just as the livestock's continued existence depended on the abilities of the farmer, sometimes the farmer's existence depended on the loyalties and genius of his animals. And just as the hardships of the Plains life hardened the farmer, so also did the rigors of the Plains seem to temper the muscles and brains of the beast. For example:

"A rancher in Brown County [Nebraska] had a horse so fast he lots of time got some place before he left home. He was a good cattle horse and found cattle even before they became lost."[8]

On the Plains it became just as important that a mount be able to stop as well as go. The cutting horse, with his back-wrenching stops and starts, is a magnificent example of this development, which apparently started early in the pioneer days: "My grandfather's mule wasn't a stubborn one, as most are. Grandfather had him so well trained that when he said, 'Whoa,' he would stop immediately, no matter how fast he was going. One day while out hunting wild game he was suddenly pursued by Indians on horseback. They had him almost surrounded and his only escape was over a very high cliff. Not hesitating he spurred the mule on over. Three feet from the rocky bottom Grandfather yelled, 'Whoa!' The mule stopped dead still. Grandfather jumped off and neither was hurt one bit."[9]

Mules have a way of lending themselves well, apparently, to the medium of the folktale. Like the traveling salesman, they just seem to fit in somehow. The *Omaha Bee,* an early, now dead, newspaper had two stories in its 1875 volume that smack of folklore. But folklore or not, they are worth recounting:

"An industrious citizen, who lives not over a thousand miles from town, arose a few mornings ago while the festive lark was still snoring and with a tin bucket under his arm went to the barn to milk the family cow. It was dark and rainy, and fumbling about for old brindle, he got into the wrong pew and began to pull the off-mule of his wagon team. He can't remember now which side of the roof he went out but his recollection of alighting on the picket fence is very vivid. He expects the bucket down in a few days."[10]

There can be no doubt that the fact of that matter has been embroidered with editorial license, but anyone who has been personally acquainted with a mule will testify that his muscle and temperament both will equip him for that kind—or this kind—of performance:

"A bad little boy near Lincoln [Nebraska] lit a pack of shooting-crackers and threw them into the street to see them 'go off.' One of Ike Hateman's mules came along and swallowed them before they 'went off.' The mule walked about fifteen feet and stopped. Things weren't acting right inside. He began to taste the smoke of fire-crackers. He laid his left ear around against his ribs and heard something. It was them crackers having fun. The mule picked out about three and a half miles of straight road and started. A [man] met him about a mile the other side of the alms-house, going south, white with perspiration, with streams of smoke shooting out of his nostrils, mouth and ears, while his tail stuck straight up, and a stream of blue and green smoke followed about ten or twelve feet in the rear. Ike found his mule yesterday morning stuck halfway through a farmhouse near Waverly, still smoking. The man [who lived in the house] had got his family out and put 'em up into a lot of trees. Ike hauled his mule home, when he got cool enough, on a dray, The man is going to move his house further back off the road, and his wife and oldest daughter will be baptized when the water gets warm. "[11]

H. C. McKelvie of Dodge County, Nebraska, had a bull that became a celebrity, very nearly a legend:

"H. C. McKelvie once told me that if I would come to his farm he would show me the fastest bull in the world. He said the bull had the habit of racing with the fast mail train every day for seven miles, the length of his pasture.

"I told Claude I was coming out sometime to see the race. The day I drove out, Claude was away and Mrs. McKelvie told me that he had left that morning for New York by way of St. Louis and was coming back by way of Omaha, but she was looking for him any minute. I thought he was covering a lot of territory in a short space of time and I asked her how he went.

"'Why,' she said, 'he rode his bull!'"[12]

Not long after this story appeared in the *Nebraska Farmer*, Marion Hannah of Brown County wrote indignantly that McKelvie's bull was actually a mere run-of-the-mill Plains bull:

"After admiring a thousand head of Herefords on one ranch in Brown County I noticed one bull that had his face bespattered with mud. I asked why just one of the thousand head should have a muddy face and the owner told me that this one had been a pet calf and used to chase him around the large two-hundred ton haystacks in that county. The bull had persisted in the practice after he had grown up and had now acquired such speed that he would chase himself around those large haystacks so fast that he would kick mud in his own face. Now, maybe Claude McKelvie's bull can show speed on a straight track, but I'd like to see these two animals race around a Brown County haystack!"[13]

All stock is noted for its strange appetites, and it is theorized that the animals are searching for nutrients that are missing from their natural feeds. One must wonder what kind of vitamins were needed by the calf described by the farmer who "nailed cardboard on the inside of his calf shed to keep out the cold winds and the calf ate it off. The next day he covered the cracks with a roll of tar paper, and that evening he finished the chores just as the calf was finishing eating the last of that roll of tar paper! The calf grew and was healthy, however. It, nor any of its offspring, was ever bothered by lice, itch, or flies. Its granddaughters never grew any hair and each one gave two gallons of tar every day instead of milk."[14]

Since the animals seemed ready to eat about anything anyway, it was only a matter of time until some farmer figured out a way to take advantage of this strange inclination:

"Unlike Lawrence Russel's uncle, we find it uneconomical to feed sawdust, and we are raising our calves on a ration which has more feeding value than sawdust on account of its variety, and the cost of production is practically nothing. Every farmer has noticed how ravenously a calf will chew a stray piece of paper. . . .[We are] feeding our calves mail order catalogs. To teach them, we first tear out the sheet which has the picture of the calf eating calf meal. He eats this page readily. Next we give him the tonic page, and after that he will eat any page in the catalog. Our calves are all doing fine, and receive nothing but catalogs, ultra-violet rays, and water. We lost one calf and after a post-mortem examination discovered it had eaten the fire-arms page, and one of the guns was loaded. If any farmer tries this method, he must be sure to tear out the fire-arms and ammunition pages."[15]

Other means have been tried to increase production on the Plains, some less successful than others: "You've heard that soft music soothes the bovine herd and prepares them for an easier milking period, but our neighbor, Old Jack, decided one cold February morning that he could get even better results with heat. He took his wife's heating pad and with the help of some scotch tape he applied it to his favorite milk cow's undercarriage. Sure enough the old Holstein gave an extra gallon of fresh warm milk, and he only had the heating pad on a low position.

"So Jack, thinking he'd found a way to revolutionize the dairy business, decided to experiment even further. Next morning he turned the heating pad to medium and sure enough the old Holstein gave two extra gallons of milk. He kept this up for several days and (ladies, you know how men are—never satisfied) so Jack being no exception turned the heating pad to high position. Now, everyone knows what happens when you apply too much heat to moisture: You're bound to get a reaction and in this case it was in the form of steam. When Jack went into the barn that poor old Holstein was a-bellerin' like a hungry calf and a-kickin', and the spigots on her undercarriage were a-spewin' off like the pop off valves on a pressure cooker.

"That's about all there is to this story except that the heat dried the cow up and Jack had to buy a new heating pad. I guess there is a moral to all this: 'If you think you've got it in the bag, don't get too steamed up about it.' "[16]

A similar unintentional effort at increased production had a surprising result—but there is no indication in the original account whether the farmer in question considered the by-products a step in the right direction:

"According to one newspaper account in 1897, a man in Dodge County [Nebraska] went into his cow stable one night and mixed up the animal a nice mash in a bowl, full of sawdust instead of bran. The cow, really supposing that hard times had come and they were all going to economize, meekly ate her supper, and the man never discovered his mistake until the next morning when the cow let down a half gallon of turpentine, a quart of shoe pegs, and a bundle of lath."[17]

A Nebraskan told with some admiration about the cleverness of Missouri's razorback hogs that had learned to keep the mosquitos off by "running back and forth through knotholes in the fence."[18]

Of all the livestock tall tales I have encountered, however, the next has touched me most deeply, because of the incredible determination shown by the plucky beast:

"I once had a goat that was very fond of butting. He would butt anything that came in his way. One evening we decided to have some fun and so we stacked up a pile of bricks and tied the goat near enough to it so that he could reach it easily. After time his head was all battered, worn out, and at last it disappeared. Soon his shoulders and front legs were gone. We went to bed and in the morning when I looked out of my window, the goat had completely disappeared except his tail and that was still butting up against the pile of bricks."[19]

SNAKES

Certainly the most infamous of Plains snakes was the hoopsnake, which unfortunately has apparently become extinct.

"The rattlesnakes have always been talked about as being a menace. The hoopsnakes were far more of a menace, were more numerous, more poisonous, and more dangerous. A fully grown hoopsnake was about twelve feet long. They took their tail in their mouth and rolled like a hoop and struck their victim with a horn in their head.

"I once saw a hoopsnake strike a large cottonwood tree. In fifteen minutes all the leaves had withered. Another time I saw one strike a fence post. In ten minutes the barbed wire, where stapled to the post, had rusted and fallen apart."[20]

That account suggests that we can be glad that the hoopsnake has gone the way of the passenger pigeon. A friend of mine used to say, "Reminds me of a girl I once went out with."

In a later letter, Ray Harpham added a footnote to the story of the rise and fall of the Plains hoopsnake:

"The reason hoopsnakes became extinct was because the

males rolled clockwise and the females rolled counterclock-
wise." That *would* explain their disappearance.

Kansas Folklore also includes a story about a hoopsnake
and its marvelous ability upon being hit to disintegrate into
several pieces which crawl off independently and then later
rejoin.[21] It might also be a subspecies of hoopsnake which
Mattes located in an early typescript by George McCowen;
this varmint was doubly dangerous, for, according to Mc-
Cowen, it had a head at both ends.[22]

Despite Mr. Dutcher's disclaimer, the rattlesnake did apparently pose a formidable danger on the Plains during the
pioneer years. Many old-timers have told me about rattlesnakes in their fury striking at hoe handles, which then swelled up to the size of telephone poles. "One such indiscriminate
snake nearly caused a disaster when he struck at Custer
Joe's off-horse one day and hit the wagon-tongue instead.
The tongue swelled up and broke the neck-yoke ring and
Joe had to chop it off to save the wagon."[23]

Wyatt's "So-Called Tall Tales About Kansas" includes
four snake tales. John Glover tells about the time a copper-
head struck a hoe handle, which then swelled to the size of
a large log. The log was milled and used to build a corn-
crib, but unfortunately the turpentine of the paint took the
swelling out of the wood, reducing the crib to such a size
that it was finally used as a dog house.[24]

Mr. Ray Harpham tells about the same kind of disaster,
except in his memory the snake struck a man's pegleg. It
swelled to the point that there was enough lumber when it
was milled to build a nice house. When the turpentine took
the swelling out of that wood, the house was used for a bird
house.

Anyone familiar with rattlers will tell you how that swelling
can spread until the whole being is infected, or for that matter. . .

"Well, sir, it seems that this mean rattlesnake hauled off and hit a telephone pole. The phones on that telephone line all swelled up so big you couldn't get in a room with 'em. After that swelling went down, they buzzed instead of ringing. That is where the expression 'Why don't you give me a buzz?' comes from. "[25]

Charles Woolf, again in Wyatt's Kansas article, tells about the time a ball of frozen rattlers were encountered while some trees were being cleared. He riled them with his axe and in their angry slashing and thrashing they cleared eighty acres of timber. [26]

It seems hard to believe anything good about rattlesnakes, but it could be that they only live up to their bad reputations. Given half a chance, they might just be useful citizens:

"Mr. Lintelman said that he had an uncle living in Wyoming who found a large rattlesnake fastened under a rock one day. His uncle took pity on the snake and released it. The snake followed him home and became a great pet and watched things around the house like a regular watch dog. One night the uncle was awakened by the sound of labored breathing and investigating he found that the snake was coiled around a burglar's throat and had its tail out of the window rattling for the police. "[27]

On another occasion some fence builders ran across a large nest of dormant rattlesnakes and since they were frozen stiff, the construction men simply drove them into the ground, much like iron posts, to hang the barbed wire on. Again misfortune struck, however, and a sudden shift in temperatures thawed the snakes. They were, it is said, last seen crawling along towards Texas dragging the shiny new wire, "and they weren't losing any time leaving the county. "[28]

Finally, Wyatt records a tale about the ingenuity of the rattler. During a particularly bad drought, a band of snakes devised the idea of forming a chain to reach the bottom of the well for a drink, each taking his drink in turn. [29]

FISH

All fishermen are liars and some pioneers were fishermen:

"In a nearby lake I liked to fish. One day I caught a fish that was so big I had to go for the neighbors to get it out of the water and into the wagon. We took it home and there being no scale large enough in the neighborhood to weigh it, we got a block and tackle and hung it on the windmill tower while I took a picture of it. That picture weighed twelve pounds."[30]

Thomas Tibbles, in his early memoirs of Plains pioneer life, notes: "I've seen the Platte fish swallow a man many a time."[31]

A Nebraskan tells this one about a Missouri fisherman:

"The fisherman felt something scraping the bottom of the boat. It was only a little row boat with about a thirty-inch beam. He looked over the port side and saw one eye looking at him; he looked over the starboard side and saw the other eye looking at him. From the distance between the eyes, he decided he was on top of a pretty fair size fish. Of course, I could believe this about Nebraska fish, but I doubt this Missouri version."[32] Since the current record-size blue catfish — 87 pounds, 8 ounces — was pulled from the Missouri River, that skepticism might be unwarranted; that big fish probably just washed down to Missouri from Nebraska.

Like the rattlesnakes, these fish were not only big — they were also exceedingly clever. Wyatt found a tale about a farmer who during a severe drought trained his fish, bit by bit, to do without water. They became so adept at it that they would spend the whole day on dry land, eating with the chickens. As seems to have been the case so often with these arrangements, however, the fish were caught out in the farmyard one day by a sudden rainstorm and they all drowned.[33]

Sadder even than this Kansas version is the following

story; perhaps I am touched by it because of the clear patriotic element in the tragedy: Alfred H. Ulrich of Wayne County, Nebraska was caught in one of those typical Plains storms we often hear about that followed him home from town so close "that, although not one drop of water fell on him as he sat in the buggy, the hind wheels were running in six inches of water. . . .

"When he got home he found a fish in the back end of his buggy. He put it in a jar to keep it for a pet but soon got tired of changing the water for it every day and he decided that it could live without water. He poured out a little of the water every day until the fish finally was used to living on dry land. Then he kept it in the canary cage and after a few meals of canary seed it could whistle like a bird and seemed to be perfectly happy.

"One day, however, when the radio set was tuned in on an orchestra that was playing the Star Spangled Banner, the poor fish tried to stand up and fell into the drinking water, and before Mr. Ulrich would reach it, it had drowned. The poor fish!"[34]

In addition to the sorrow which all readers must also feel, I cannot help but wonder if the fish in the Kansas story, eating chicken feed as they were, were ever induced to lay eggs in a nest.

As the wild fish acquired their share of wiliness, they applied their knowledge in the never-ending struggle against crafty Plains fishermen: "A man was fishing when a huge fish got on his line. It was so big in fact that he called for help. A skindiver not far away heard his call and went to see if he might be of help. The fisherman suggested he dive down and see how large the fish was. He went down and soon came back with the report 'that it was a very large fish, but that it swam inside an old car body and so lodged there. Picking up a stick, the fisherman asked if he would please dive down and poke him out with the stick. The skindiver took the stick and disappeared into the water. When he returned to the fisherman he reported that he had no luck, for everytime he tried to give the fish a poke with the stick, he'd roll up the windows on the car."[35]

As was also the case with the rattlesnakes, pioneers found that fish, given half a chance, could prove to be compassionate, sensitive, and grateful fellow-creatures:

"W. Harrison Stephens of Nuckolls County tells of a fishing trip which he took on the Cedar River two years ago. 'I caught a four-foot bass, but upon seeing the appealing look in the fish's eyes I promptly threw it back into the water. When I reached home, I discovered the loss of a valuable watch.

"'Two years passed by and I returned to the same river. While idly casting my line into the water I noticed a large bass circling about the boat. Suspecting something, I waited, and to my surprise the fish brought my lost watch to the surface. The watch was running! Marks on the stem indicated that the faithful bass had daily wound the watch and it was only five minutes slow.' "[36]

I once had much the same experience while fishing on the Loup River near Fullerton, Nebraska. I too lost a fine German watch and fully expected that it was gone forever. About two years later, while boating on that river with some colleagues, I caught (to their envy) a fine 22-inch catfish, with much the same look on his face as the one I had set free on the fishing trip two years earlier. Imagine my surprise when opening him the next morning for breakfast to find a complete set of entrails.

BIRDS

White tells about a farmer who moved so often that his chickens got so that they would roll over on their backs and cross their legs to be tied for a move every time the wagon was rolled into the yard.[37]

Every effort was made to help chickens adapt to the rigors of the Plains. In the song, "Sweet Nebraska Land," we hear:

> Our chickens are so very poor,
> They beg for crumbs outside our door.[38]

And it was by way of alleviating the scarcity of feed that one pioneer "fed his chickens on sawdust and corn meal until they became so big and strong that he was afraid of them, and then he cut the corn meal out of the ration and fed them the sawdust alone.

"Uncle got his tongue full of splinters from eating the eggs and contracted wooditis. One of his hens laid a knot hole. He set some of these eggs and hatched out a battery of cross-grained woodpeckers. The only way he could cook the chickens was after boiling them in wood alcohol."

The editors of the *Nebraska Farmer*, unable to let a story like that set (or perhaps I should say "lay") remarked:

"This story reminds us of the bright young lady from the business college who said that she supposed the old hen would soon no longer be necessary with the incubators and brooders that are in use nowadays. E. DeFord of Bellwood, Nebraska, tells us of his hen that began laying when three weeks old. In December she decided to set and hatched eighteen chicks out of as many eggs and laid a double-yoked egg every day while she was setting and only left the nest long enough to bring it to the house."[39]

I believed that Mr. DeFord had *some* chicken when I first read that story, but as usual Ray Harpham had one better. A chicken dumb enough to haul an egg to the house every day doesn't look too good beside those of the farmer who "crossed his hens with a parrot. It worked fine. They would come and tell him where they laid their eggs. But two hens were liars (imagine that!) and he ran his legs off looking for their nests."

It was a tough life for man *and* bird, but they say that

some of those pioneer chickens grew up so tough on a diet of grasshoppers that it took only eight of their eggs to make a dozen.[40]

Civilization also brought new skills and knowledge to the wild birds. Anyone who has ever hunted pheasants around here has lost whatever doubt he might have had about that bird's brain, for they apparently keep good track of the calendar: they can be seen by the dozens, parading around and generally getting under foot—until the pheasant season opens, during which you literally have to rout them out of their nests with an auger.

"The pheasants were once so thick up there [in Greeley County, Nebraska] that they were damaging the corn. They even dug up the newly planted kernels. They say that the old rooster pheasants became so smart that they had figured out the check-row corn planter, took so many steps, scratched up the kernel, took the same number of steps, dug up another kernel, and so on."[41]

The situation is clearly at a critical stage when the editors of a liars' contest have to admit that one of the entries is "untrue," but that is exactly what was said of the following effort:

"A farmer met a city student and thought he would act as though he was green. He pointed to a crow on a rail and remarked that that bird had been imported from Spain and could whistle 'Home Sweet Home' so beautifully that it made tears run down his beak.

"The city student replied that that was no accomplishment because he once had a crow that could whistle 'The Village Blacksmith' so naturally that the sparks would fly from the end of its tail."

The judges concluded that the story must be false "because 'The Village Blacksmith' is a poem and not a song and we cannot give Mr. Zvolanek a prize on that account."[42]

RABBITS

George B. Mair, editor of the *Callaway Courier*, had the 19th-century editor's turn of wit and he used it freely. In poking fun at his mythical small Nebraska town of Podunk, he told a few tales about the local "jack":

"A brindle dog with one ear came to town last Monday and viciously attacked one champion high jumper of the Podunk Athletic Club, Jack Rabbitson, injuring him so seriously that a match he had arranged with a claim jumper from Stop Table had to be postponed."

And on another occasion, "The late sleet storm made the grass on our sidewalks so slippery that one of our prominent jackrabbits fell and sprained one of his ankles so badly that he walks with a limp."[43] Grass on the sidewalks?

There are plenty of stories about cowboys trying to get a rope on a jack rabbit and ride him and there are an equal number of stories about the broken legs resulting from the falls, but the following tale is the best, in my estimation:

"One hot and dry summer, Grandpa hired a *kid* from town, about 19 years old, (in those days all males were called 'kid' 'til they were at least 25 years old or over) for to herd the sheep along the roads and other waste places where there were still a few spears of grass. Hired the kid for board and room. Grandpa and his two sons were busy trying to harvest their meager wheat and oats crop. Grandpa had a fairly large stock shed for the cattle and sheep. Pole and straw roof. 'Air conditioned.' So he instructed the kid, 'Be sure you get all the sheep in the shed for the night and close the door tight so no coyote can get at them.'

"At the supper table Grandpa asked the kid, 'Well, how did you get along with the sheep? Did you get them all in the shed?'

"'Oh I got along just fine,' the kid replied. 'There's lots of good picking at some spots, but I had quite a time getting that one lamb in the shed, but I finally got it in.'

"'Lamb? Why, there's not a lamb in the bunch.'

"'Oh, yes sir, there is, and I got it penned up with the rest.'

"'This I got to see,' remarked Grandpa. So they went out and into the shed.

"'There it is,' said the kid pointing towards one corner in the shed. And darned if there wasn't one of them large Nebraska white-tailed jack-rabbits crouched in the corner."[44]

The jack rabbit—originally called the "jack-ass rabbit"—excited the curiosity and comment of a good many Plains travellers who were used to the less spectacular eastern rabbits and European hares, but no one described him as well as Mark Twain, who crossed Nebraska during his trip west in the early 1860s:

"As the sun was going down, we saw the first specimen of an animal known familiarly over two thousand miles of mountain and desert—from Kansas clear to the Pacific Ocean—as the "jackass rabbit." He is well named. He is just like any other rabbit, except that he is from one third to twice as large, has longer legs in proportion to his size, and has the most preposterous ears that ever were mounted on any creature *but* a jackass. When he is sitting quiet, thinking about his sins, or is absent-minded or unapprehensive of danger, his majestic ears project above him conspicuously; but the breaking of a twig will scare him nearly to death, and then he tilts his ears back gently and starts for home. All you can see, then, for the next minute, is his long gray form stretched out straight and 'streaking it' through the low sage-brush, head erect, eyes right, and ears just canted a little to the rear, but showing you where the animal is, all the time, the same as if he carried a jib. Now and then he makes a marvelous spring with his long legs, high over the stunted sage-brush, and scores a leap that would make a horse envious. Presently he comes down to a long, graceful 'lope,' and shortly he mysteriously disappears. He has crouched behind a sage-brush, and will sit there and listen and tremble until you get within six feet of him, when he will get under way again. But one must shoot at this creature once, if he wishes to see him throw his heart into his heels, and do the best he knows how. He is frightened clear through, now, and he lays his long ears down his back, straightens himself out like a yard-stick every spring he makes, and scatters miles behind him with an easy indifference that is enchanting. . . at a speed which can only be described as a flash and a vanish! Long after he was out of sight we could hear him whiz. "[45]

DOGS AND CATS

Nearly a third of the 800 sod-house photographs from pioneer times on the Plains that I examined in preparing *Sod Walls* showed a dog frequently included in the portrait as a part of the family circle. Who knows how many more were off chasing rabbits or snakes—far too busy to spend time in the idleness of photography—or how many were locked up inside the shed so that they would not shred the photographer's pants. At any rate, the dog was an integral part of the working pioneer family, and predictably he also had his part in the tall tales of the time:

"If the possibilities of sweet clover were known, many acres in south-central Nebraska would be seeded to this so-called roadside pest. One fall while I was repairing fences near a patch of sweet clover, my Scotch Collie dog took a dip in the creek and when he came out he started after a rabbit, chasing him into the clover patch. The next spring the clover started to grow upon his back, with a perfect stand.

"Three spring calves followed him around all summer picking the green plants, and the only time the dog objected was when they picked it so close they pulled his hair.

"The next summer I placed him in an enclosure with a hive of bees and I took sixty-two pounds of honey from the hive and harvested nearly two bushels of seed in the fall. "[46]

The following story about a rather remarkable dog won a 1970 tall-tale contest sponsored by the *Custer County Chief* in Broken Bow, Nebraska.

"My mother was raised in the wooded country of southern Iowa. The settlers there in those early days had very little in the way of entertainment, except perhaps the fun of spinning yarns around the pot-bellied stove in the old country store, about their kids, their mules, and their hound-dogs. She used to tell this one that she remembered having heard on one of these occasions, as told by one of the most notorious of these tall-tale tellers.

"'One day me an' my houn'-dog Zeke was out in the woods a-huntin' fer rabbits. We was a-runnin' powerful short of meat that spring an' Zeke he knew as well as I did that it was purty important we git one or we better not go home. We had poked out all the briar patches and tromped through the wild plum thickets and was a-gittin' purty discouraged cuz we hadn't seen hide ner hair of a rabbit yit. I set down clost by a saplin' fer to rest a spell, but Zeke wasn't tard yit, so he wandered on out into the woods and wuz gone so long I was wunderin' what become of him, when all at onct here come a rabbit licketysplit outa the thicket right towards me, and right behind him come Zeke jest a-tarin' up the airth behind 'im, he was a-runnin' so fast. The rabbit darted past me an' the saplin', an' tore for a briar patch about a hunnert feet away. Now I always knew Zeke was a mighty smart dawg an' I knew he's figger out some way to gain on that rabbit before it got to the briar patch. Well, Zeke never took time to go around the saplin'; he hit it head on and at sech speed that the saplin' split that houn'-dawg clean in two, from the tip of his nose to the end of his tail. Right quick like I grabbed up the two halves and slapped them together again, only in my haste I got two legs up and two legs down. Well, that never hindered Zeke at all. He jest kept on a-runnin', turnin' over and over like a cartwheel, an' he caught that rabbit jest two jumps short of the briar patch.'"[47]

This next tale is one that clearly testifies to the dedication and faithfulness, strength and pluck of the noble family dog:

"This dog was half water spaniel and Irish setter. One day when I was fishing, my dog was sitting by my side looking into the water. All at once he dived into the creek and out of sight. I thought he was drowned. About fifteen minutes later I heard a dog barking a quarter of a mile down the stream, and saw to my surprise there were ten catfish and eight bass which my dog had treed.

"This dog was good to hunt chickens with also. Whenever he found birds he just held them until I could come to shoot them. We had a thirty-acre field of bluestem grass in which my brother and I were hunting. My dog set some chickens but the grass was so tall we could not find him. We gave it up and went home thinking the dog would follow soon. He didn't come, and so the next day we decided we would have to find the dog to keep him from starving to death, because we knew he would hold those chickens until he died. We couldn't find him and we finally decided to burn the field and drive him out that way. When the fire died down there was my dog, holding a chicken about thirty feet from him, both burned to a crisp. I'd like to have a dog like that again."[48]

Sometimes the ability of these pioneer dogs not only to hold but to detect quarry was absolutely uncanny:

"There was once a guy who had a dog he was very proud of. He would hold a point on any bird for any length of time. He was in a bar with the dog and the dog suddenly jumped up and went into a point at another guy who had just walked into the bar. The dog's owner looked around and could not see anything that might have caused the dog's behavior. He asked the man, 'Do you happen to have a bird in your pocket?'

"'No,' he answered.

"'Have you been hunting recently? Could you have the scent of a bird on you somehow?'

"'No.'

"'Well, I am certainly sorry my dog is behaving like this,'

the dog's owner apologized. 'I hope that it hasn't embarrased you too much, Mr. . . ? Mr. . . ?'

"'Partridge,' the man answered."[49]

This story about dogs appeared in the *Omaha World-Herald*, repeated from the *Transcript*, a Bayard, Nebraska, newspaper:

"The week hasn't been a total loss. A salesman came to the house the other night while I was trying to give one of my cussed dogs a little training.

"'Sit,' says I. The dog must have been tired. Anyway, it sat.

"'That's pretty good,' said the salesman. 'Does he (dern fool couldn't even tell it wasn't a he) do anything else?'

"'Just one other.'

"'Show me.'

"'Sic 'em.'"

Another newspaper editor, George Mair of the *Callaway Courier*, made what I consider to be a fine appraisal of another canine, the coyote:

"What he lacks in beauty is more than made up in ugliness."[50]

But again Samuel L. Clemens[51] does his contemporaries one better. His description of the coyote stands without parallel:

"Along about an hour after breakfast we saw the first prairie-dog villages, the first antelope, and the first wolf. If I remember rightly, this latter was the regular *coyote* (pronounced ky-*o*-te) of the farther deserts. And if it *was*, he was not a pretty creature or respectable either, for I got well acquainted with his race afterward, and can speak with confidence. The coyote is a long, slim, sick and sorry-looking skeleton, with a gray wolf-skin stretched over it, a tolerably bushy tail that forever sags down with a despairing expression of forsakenness and misery, a furtive and evil eye, and a long, sharp face, with slightly lifted lip and exposed teeth. He has a general slinking expression all over. The coyote is a living, breathing allegory of Want. He is *always* hungry. He is always poor, out of luck and friendless. The meanest creatures despise him, and even the fleas would desert him for a veloc- ipede. He is so spiritless and cowardly that even while his exposed teeth are pretending a threat, the rest of his face is apologizing for it. And he is *so* homely!—so scrawny, and ribby, and coarse-haired, and pitiful. When he sees you he lifts his lip and gets a flash of his teeth out, and then turns a little out of the course he was pursuing, depresses his head a bit, and strikes a long, soft-footed trot through the sage- brush, glancing over his shoulder at you, from time to time, till he is about out of easy pistol range, and then he stops and takes a deliberate survey of you; he will trot fifty yards and stop again—another fifty yards and stop again; and fi- nally the gray of his gliding body blends with the gray of the sage-brush, and he disappears. All this is when you make no demonstration against him; but if you do, he develops a livelier interest in his journey, and instantly electrifies his heels and puts such a deal of real estate between himself and your weapon, that by the time you have raised the hammer you see that you need a minie rifle, and by the time you have got him in line you need a rifled cannon, and by the time you have 'drawn a bead' on him you see well enough that nothing but an unusually long-winded streak of light- ning could reach him where he is now. But if you start a swift-footed dog after him, you will enjoy it ever so much— especially if it is a dog that has a good opinion of himself, and has been brought up to think he knows something about speed.

"The cayote will go swinging gently off on that deceitful trot of his, and every little while he will smile a fraudful smile over his shoulder that will fill that dog entirely full of encouragement and worldly ambition, and make him lay his head still lower to the ground, and stretch his neck fur- ther to the front, and pant more fiercely, and stick his tail out straighter behind and move his furious legs with a yet wilder frenzy, and leave a broader and broader, and higher and denser cloud of desert sand smoking behind, and mark-

ing his long wake across the level plain! And all this time
the dog is only a short twenty feet behind the cayote, and to
save the soul of him he cannot understand why it is that he
cannot get perceptibly closer; and he begins to get aggrava-
ted, and it makes him madder and madder to see how gently
the cayote glides along and never pants or sweats or ceases
to smile; and he grows still more and more incensed to see
how shamefully he has been taken in by an entire stranger,
and what an ignoble swindle that long, calm, soft-footed trot
is; and next he notices that he is getting fagged, and that
the cayote actually has to slacken speed a little to keep from
running away from him—and *then* that town-dog is mad in
earnest, and he begins to strain and weep and swear, and
paw the sand higher than ever, and reach for the cayote
with concentrated and desperate energy. This 'spurt' finds him
six feet behind the gliding enemy, and two miles from his
friends. And then, in the instant that a wild new hope is
lighting upon his face, the cayote turns and smiles blandly
upon him once more, and with a something about it which
seems to say: 'Well, I shall have to tear myself away from
you, bub—business is business, and it will not do for me to
be fooling along this way all day'—and forthwith there is a
rushing sound, and the sudden splitting of a long crack
through the atmosphere, and behold that dog is solitary and
alone in the midst of a vast solitude!

"It makes his head swim. He stops, and looks all around;
climbs the nearest sand-mound, and gazes into the distance;
shakes his head reflectively, and then, without a word, he
turns and jogs back to his train, and takes up a humble
position under the hindmost wagon, and feels unspeakably
mean, and looks ashamed, and hangs his tail at half-mast
for a week. And for as much as a year after that, whenever
there is a great hue and cry after a cayote, that dog will
merely glance in that direction without emotion, and apparently observe to himself, 'I believe I do not wish any of the
pie.'

"The cayote lives chiefly in the most desolate and forbidden deserts, along with the lizard, the jackass-rabbit and the raven, and gets an uncertain and precarious living, and earns it. He seems to subsist almost wholly on the carcases of oxen, mules and horses that have dropped out of emigrant trains and died, and upon windfalls of carrion, and occasional legacies of offal bequeathed to him by white men who have been opulent enough to have something better to butcher than condemned army bacon. . . .

"He does not mind going a hundred miles to breakfast, and a hundred and fifty to dinner, because he is sure to have three or four days between meals, and he can just as well be travelling and looking at the scenery as lying around doing nothing and adding to the burdens of his parents.

"We soon learned to recognize the sharp, vicious bark of the cayote as it came across the murky plain at night to disturb our dreams among the mail-sacks; and remembering his forlorn aspect and his hard fortune, made shift to wish him the blessed novelty of a long day's good luck and a limitless larder the morrow."

I have found only one tall tale about pioneer cats, but what it lacks in number and length, it more than makes up in mind bending:

"Cats? A big old tomcat was a chicken killer, so they killed him eight times. He did it again, so they cut off his head but he came back carrying it in his mouth."[52]

INSECTS

Dogs and cats, even wives and children, can be ignored, taken for granted occasionally, out-argued, or abandoned, but insects have a way of extracting the instant and constant attention of any man they care to deal with. It is not surprising then that a good number of tales developed about the littlest and in many ways most troublesome of Plains critters: insects. They even found their way into the pioneer folksongs—for example, in "Starving to Death on a Government Claim":

> Hurrah for Lane County, the land of the free,
> The home of the grasshopper, bedbug, and flea;
> I'll holler its praises and sing of its fame,
> While starving to deat. on a government claim.[53]

Even in song the stories about insects seemed larger than life. A couplet in "Bugs and Fleas" complains (or brags):

> 'Twas just the other day I found
> A great big flea that weighed five pound.[54]

Pioneers complained that mosquitos got so much of their blood that they felt inclined to consider them relatives, but they were far too hostile to be considered friends. The most popular of mosquito tales, told in many versions, including one Febold Feboldson tale, was told to me in this fashion by a man whose grandfather had been a blacksmith and to whom this really happened, he said:

"One night the mosquitos, drawn to the light of his forge, became intolerable. Finally, he tried to escape them by crawling under a huge iron kettle sitting upside down in the forge shed. To his amazement, those Nebraska skeeters drilled their stingers right through the iron kettle.

"But he remained calm and used his hammer to bend over the stingers as they poked through the kettle bottom. Eventually, however, after he had bent over 15 or 20 stingers, those mosquitos just flew off with the kettle—and grandfather decided to call it an evening."[55]

Another Nebraskan had a similar experience in Canada, but he had the good fortune to find the kettle several miles from the lumber camp where he was working several days later. He and some of the other laborers in the camp used the punctured kettle as a soup strainer and whenever it rained they would hoist it up into the trees and use it as a shower bath.[56]

That story is enough to make me uneasy about going outside on a summer evening, but the next one is certain to give you bad dreams:

"One terrified homesteader awoke to see two huge figures standing in his doorway. He quickly recognized them to be mosquitos. The one said, 'Shall we eat him here or take him with us?'

"The other replied, 'We better eat him here. If we take him along the big guys will take him away from us when we get home.'"[57]

Some events of "The Grasshopper Years" are so incredible that they would be hard to believe even if they were not appearing here in the middle of all these other lies, but I submit as fact that there were times when the grasshoppers became so thick on the railroad tracks that locomotives could not pass and line workers had to be called in to shovel and sand the tracks.[58] Clouds of grasshoppers actually did darken the skies so that the chickens went to roost.

Turnips were eaten down into the ground and the bark was eaten from young trees. Harness and clothes were shredded. The 'hoppers gnawed the binding twine on shocks and then devoured the grain.[59] Tool handles were made rough where the invincible mandibles ate away the soft parts of the wood. One pioneer newspaper editor turned his gymnastic tongue to describe the prodigious and indiscriminate palate of the grasshopper:

"While a healthy ox may be a very fair, steady-gaited digester, there is no comparison between the slow assimilating process of his burley bread basket and the quick electric stomach machinery of the speedy and voracious grasshopper. A sound, valid member of this nomadic family of gluttons can eat, digest, and extrude three times his own weight in green corn, four times his bulk in peaches, without sugar or cream, six times his stature in raw turnips, four pounds of green tobacco, and a peck of onions every twenty-four hours. And radishes, which are quite trying on the ordinary stomach, digests as a calf does milk. "[60]

I am somewhat less certain about the verity of the oft-told tale about the farmer who left his team to walk the fields one day and return to find that grasshoppers had eaten the team and wagon and were pitching the horseshoes to see which ones got to eat the harness. [61]

Mari Sandoz has some of her characters discussing the grasshopper problem in her *Son of the Gamblin' Man*:

"'Yes,' Sam Atkinson added softly. 'I hear that up on the Niobrara River the hoppers are so thick they're damming the whole 300-foot-deep canyon, dropping pebbles in, to flood the country and grow their own greenstuff.' "[62]

As I have mentioned before, newspaper editors had their own flair for language and the style of the land. Over-statement could be devastatingly funny too, as, for example, when the editor of one Kansas newspaper, during the worst of the grasshopper storms, when everything was either covered or filled with the detested 'hoppers, noted at the head of a front-page story, "A Grasshopper Was Seen On The Courthouse Steps!"[63]

One ingenious Kansan filled his corn planter as if he were planting corn for all he was worth. The grasshoppers congregated from miles around to wait for the crop to come up, but the wily farmer had shut off the planting mechanism and the grasshoppers sat there and starved to death waiting.[64]

Another Kansas farmer recorded that beekeeping proved unprofitable on his farm because the workers, after flying out to the alfalfa fields, would be so loaded down with the rich harvest of nectar that they would have to walk back to the hive. He then had to use two quarts of glycerine to salve the blistered feet of those poor, foot-sore bees. But they did become so used to the treatment finally that they would lie on their backs upon returning from a day's work so that the farmer could apply the glycerine balm.[65]

Squirrels don't seem to fit into any other category and are

rather rare in Plains tall tales, since trees were rare on the Plains, but the following story is just too good to omit, even if it does defy categorization:

"Harlan Helton used to tell about his dad having a corn-crib and a large cottonwood tree right beside it. The pesky squirrels would take an ear of corn and go up the tree to eat it. He got mad and cut the tree down and it was nothing to see a squirrel run twenty-five or thirty feet into the air before he realized the tree wasn't there anymore."[66]

HARD TIMES

5

Through all the joking, tall-tale telling, and good-natured lying, there was still a thread of tragedy, for laugh as they might, a good many of those pioneers wound up dead or financially ruined or had to face the humiliation of returning to the East or Europe as failures. And throughout the tragedy there is a thread of humor. It again becomes clear that humor was not a secondary skill but an essential part of the pioneers' stamina. As I read their accounts or look at their pictures and try to transport myself to their stark and sometimes brutal existence, I find myself choked with the immensity of their courage—and what obvious results my own resolve would have found in those hard days. In their humor lies the ultimate expression of that courage.

They could even laugh about hard times: "My wife was married thirteen years before she saw a dime."[1]

Even the Crossers, those who used the Plains only as a highway to the Further West, felt the demands of the land:

One steamboat captain "ventured the guess that if all the forgotten graves were located, there would be enough to make the shores of the Missouri one continuous cemetery from its mouth to its source."[2]

Others saw the Oregon-Mormon Trail complex as one great city, a thousand miles long and one wagon wide. And diseases raced along that long city as they would in any other great city of the time. It was said that it was possible to walk from the Missouri to Fort Laramie stepping only on graves.

The accommodations of the rest ranches along the Trails were at best only adequate:

"A favorite story of the West pictured a hotel patron complaining to the landlord about the towel, whereupon that worthy, with an air of authority, squelched the patron with 'There's twenty-six men used that towel before you and you're the first one that complained.'"[3]

The provisions were none too plentiful and none too attractive at these wayside inns. A favorite joke about the situation told about a tired traveller who stopped by one such road ranch in 1864 for some water and rest; as was the custom of the time and country, he was invited to stay for a meal:

"'I don't care if I do,' quickly responded the anticipating pedestrian as he took his place at the table. The host cut off a helping of fat pork and asked the guest to pass his plate. 'Thank you,' replied the visitor, 'I never eat it.'

" 'Very well,' returned the host, 'Just help yourself to the mustard.'"[4]

Sometimes the obvious fertility of Plains soil was negated by excessive railroad costs, impossible weather, grasshoppers, or one of the myriad of other possible disasters the pioneers learned to fear. Then, although it must have been an agonizing decision, they sometimes had to turn from the soil:

"A poverty-stricken farmer . . . entered a local, small-town hardware store to buy three hammer handles at the price of one dollar each. The next week he was back to purchase eight more at the same price, and two weeks later twenty more. The hardware dealer, who had not sold more than ten hammer handles in any one year since he had opened business, finally was compelled to ask the farmer what he was doing with the handles.

"He replied, 'Selling 'em.'

" 'Well, I haven't sold that many handles in the past three years,' the shopkeeper said in wonder. 'How much are you getting for them?'

"The farmer answered, 'Fifty cents each.'

" 'But that's less than you're paying for them. You're losing fifty cents a hammer handle!'

"The farmer shrugged with resignation, 'That's a damn-sight better than I was doing when I was just a dirt-far-mer.'"5

Although my informant assured me that the next story is about hard times in Missouri, it may well be a reflection of how things were everywhere:

"You probably heard of 'poling hogs'?" I hadn't. "The hogs are so hungry for acorns that one of the chores is to tie the hogs on a long pole and hold them up the oak trees so they can get their fill of acorns." (A standard follow-up for this tall tale is, "Doesn't that take a lot of time?" and the traditional answer is, "Time don't mean nothing to hogs.")6

Mari Sandoz' works are filled with the agonies of hard times, for the Sandhills, her special area of interest, was at best a marginal farming area:

" 'Buzzard's getting so hungry they've took to following their own shadows,' Milton said in disgust."7

It is not surprising then:

"Times were so hard that the jack rabbits had to carry their own lunch."8

Or—"Times got so tough we made soup out of the pictures in the seed catalogue. Afterward we just used the whole page because we like beef soup and the articles in the catalogue were a lot of bull."8

"A great strapping Ohioan and his ample wife once set-tled on the Plains. Their first child was just a little bit of a thing. When his friends asked the big guy how that could be, that such a great big man and a great big woman could have such a small child, he said, 'When you plant a crop in Nebraska you're lucky to get back your seed.' "[10]

Sometimes it is clear when one hears or reads these stories that the humor was wearing thin. Survival and retention of the land were just too damned crucial for a really good belly laugh. One senses that, I think, in these two stories:

"The land is so plastered over with mortgages that they have to bore a hole through them with an auger before they can plant corn."

"These mortgages are necessary up in Merrick County, for . . . the wind blows so much that the only way to hold a farm down is to put a mortgage on it. Mr. Clark said that the local banker was once telling a number of men in the barber shop about buying a bottle of medicine and although it was tightly corked the hot and dusty winds had completely dried the medicine up and the bottle was full of dirt from some-body's farm—and the mortgage was still sticking to it! The banker said that he could prove this story because he still held the mortgage, and every farmer present looked sheep-ish and walked out."[11]

Then as now, the righteous injunctions to the poor that they could live better if they just took it upon themselves to improve their own lot must have been a hard pill to swallow. Already under attack from nature and the elements, his fel-low man seemed to be turning on him too. A magnificiently laconic statement of the farmer's inextricable plight came to me in the form of this story from Ray Harpham, master storyteller:

"Sometimes we didn't get much of a crop. We planted ten bushels of potatoes and raised ten bushel. It was our own fault. If we had planted more, we would have raised more."[12]

Also from Ray Harpham:

"My dad's favorite: A salesman got lost on the Plains and toward night he managed to find a farm house. He asked if he might stay all night. The farmer allowed he could, but said they didn't have much to eat. He tied his team alongside the farmer's and they sat down to supper. All there was was a large bowl of cottage cheese. When he was about half done eating, the farmer grabbed the cottage cheese and put it in the cupboard. He said, 'That's all we have for breakfast.'

"Come bed time, so the farmer told the salesman, 'As we only have one bed, my wife will get in first, I'll sleep next to her, and you can sleep on the outside.'

"About two a.m. they were awakened by an uproar. The farmer said, 'Them horses are fighting down in the stable.' He jumped out of bed and ran down to the barn.

"The farmer's wife nudged the salesman and said, 'Now's your chance.'

"So he got up and ate the rest of the cottage cheese."[13]

I don't believe I've encountered harder times than that.

One Kansas druggist had his own way of alleviating hard times. He was never out of "lard oil," or "bear oil," or even "rattlesnake oil"—because he drew them all out of the same barrel.[14]

Occasionally one gets the uneasy feeling that things just might not be getting much better either. During the past year a Nebraskan went to the bank to withdraw his life savings and the teller asked him whether he wanted it heads or tails.

OTHER PLAINS LIES

6

Among animals, one has a sense of humor.
Humor saves a few steps, it saves years.
Marianne Moore

'Tis strange but true; for truth is always
strange;
Stranger than fiction.
Lord Byron

I cannot and will not vouch for the falseness of any of
these lies. I would not be in the least surprised if some day
an indignant Nebraskan should confront me with undeniable
evidence that what I have been calling a lie is actually truth.
For the present, the reader will just have to rely on my judg-
ment, that what I say is a lie is indeed a lie. I have, you
may be sure, checked as closely as possible the inaccuracy
of the stories included in this collection.

Remember, however, that deception was not beyond the
pioneer, and he might well have passed off truth as lies:

"Some land offices were particular in requiring a house to
have glass windows. The well-known correspondent, Albert
D. Richardson, while visiting in Kansas, noticed a window
sash without panes hanging upon a nail in a settlers' cabin.
He had seen similar frames in other cabins and asked what
it was for.

"'To pre-empt with,' was the reply.

"'How?'

"'Why, don't you understand? To enable my witness to
swear that there is *a window in my house.*'"[1]

The early days of settlement were complicated by a lack

of suitable construction materials, and, for that matter, a lack of virtually everything else: Everett Dick tells of a young Kansas governor whose library consisted of one volume. But strangely enough there were times when there was a painful excess of money, much as that must sound like a tall tale. Actually, it was not so much a matter of too *much* money as it was of too many *kinds* of money.

"A captain on a Missouri steamboat came ashore to purchase wood for his steam boilers. The cautious wood seller asked about the kind of money the captain intended to use to pay for the wood, for every bank that had a door to open was issuing scrip, which as often as not was totally worthless. When the river man answered, 'The best on earth —the new Platte Valley Bank,' the wood seller replied, 'I'll trade you cord for cord.'"[2]

Despite the paucity and poverty of the Plains, every effort was made to bring and find culture wherever possible:

"The Podunk Symphony Orchestra is giving a series of delightful concerts in the Wiggle Creek opera house, which is drawing capacity crowds. A special program has been arranged for Saturday night, a feature of which will be a mixed chorus led by Howlovitch Coyote, who will be assisted by the celebrated baritone, Prof. Ole Bull Frog."[3]

No matter how small and remote the town, civic pride ran hot and high:

"A Bay Poland China cow, with her two-year-old Duroc Jersey calf, was looking over our city yesterday. We thought at first that they were looking for a good location for a dairy, but later discovered that they were residents of the old town [of Callaway], where the grass on the streets is so badly out of repair that they suffer for want of food, and had come over to Podunk to get a square meal from the up-to-date grass with which our streets are paved."

A certain number of the problems of settlement must have arisen from the European's lack of understanding of the ways and language of the frontier:

"It took us three days to make the trip [to the Cedar Canyons, where wood could be obtained] and on the way we ran across a German who was cutting sod. I asked him what he was doing and he said, 'I am yust making a chicken house for the dog first. He yust vas a goot dog, already he killed him a skunk. Ve could not stand by dat dog, so my neighbor he said, "You bury that dog for a couple of days." I yust did that but he digs out as fast as I throw the dirt in on him.' "4

Eventually, however, the immigrants acquired the ways of the West, but often they retained some little article that they had brought with them from the homeland, something to remind them of the old days and old ways. One Nebraskan told me that his father brought a grandfather clock with him from Germany and that that clock "was so old that the pendulum's shadow had worn a hole in the back of the clock case."5

Problems beyond the imagination of modern man confronted those hardy settlers. For example, digging a well. Most of us today wouldn't even know where to start. Well, the pioneers had their problems too, but they eventually mastered the skill. One man in Aurora, Nebraska told me that an old-timer in that area prided himself on digging good, straight wells, but in the beginning his excavations were so crooked that he had fallen out of his first well three times.

A similar difficulty with the water system: "In the early twenties my older brother George and I had the chore of pumping water on the days the wind didn't blow. This one day after school we had started turning the old wooden wheel and were lamenting that we had to water some fifty or sixty cows before dark. After several minutes one of us looked down to see that the tank was empty. Then we realized that we had turned the wheel backwards and we had water shooting up five or six feet from every gopher hole for a distance of half-a-mile from the well."6

By now you sense my affection and sympathy for the

pioneer. But there is one facet of his psychology that I understand all too well and for which I have very little sympathy: his attitude toward and treatment of the Indians. I am an Omaha and so I can make no pretensions of objectivity in this matter, just as I have never pretended to be objective in my manifest admiration of the pioneer. A good many of the problems were matters of cultural misunderstanding, and nothing much could have been done about that. The Omaha, for example, who had and has a system of open hospitality, understood and quickly accepted the missionaries' explanation of the Golden Rule, for that was already his way of life in terms of hospitality—but no one explained to the Indian that the Golden Rule is an *ideal,* not a *practice,* in white culture; so many a brave who strolled into a soddy, where he smelled food and assumed that hungry as he was he would be fed—just as a white would be in an Omaha village—left with a load of buckshot under his buckskins. Less understandable, however, is the pioneer's anger and distrust at the Indian's theft of his sugar, coffee, and calico, while he was in the open and brutal process of stealing the Indian's land, buffalo, and pride.

A good deal was made about the threat of Indian attack, murder, and abduction, about their easy acquisition of the white man's property. It was said of the Indians that they would, for example, steal the tires from a man's wagon wheels while he was driving at a trot.[7] And at least one pioneer had a close escape from a band of raiding Indians when, fortunately for him, a shoe from his horse flew back, hit the first of the pursuing braves, bounced on and hit the next, and then the next, and the next, until finally all five had been slain.[8]

Most of the Indian troubles took place in gossip sessions around a glowing winter stove. Less impressionable chroniclers of early Plains life take a rather cynical point of view toward the Indian danger. Mari Sandoz describes the usual course of an Indian scare:

"After the first few weeks the Panhandle [of Nebraska] treated the uprising as a joke, mostly on the Indians. When a Chadron paper noted the finding of a petrified man near a stone fence not far from town, another editor commented: 'Probably a hardened old sinner who laid down to wait for the Indian outbreak and fossilized waiting.'"[9]

Mark Twain also heard his share of Indian massacre tales when he crossed Nebraska and, although he does not exactly say so, one gets the impression that he might have had his doubts about their veracity:

"We crossed the sand hills near the scene of the Indian mail robbery and massacre of 1856, wherein the driver and conductor perished, and also all the passengers but one, it was supposed; but this must have been a mistake, for at different times afterward on the Pacific coast I was personally acquainted with a hundred and thirty-three or four people who were wounded during that massacre, and barely escaped with their lives. There was no doubt of the truth of it—I had it from their own lips.

"One of these parties told me that he kept coming across arrow-heads in his system for nearly seven years after the massacre; and another of them told me that he was stuck so literally full of arrows that after the Indians were gone and he could raise up and examine himself, he could not restrain his tears, for his clothes were completely ruined."[10]

A Nebraskan told me that his grandpap was once caught in an Indian raid and nearly died of thirst. Seems he was so poked full of holes by arrows and bullets that he wouldn't hold water any more.[11]

Like Twain, I am inclined to believe the next story, because it was apparently originally told by the man who lived through the experience:

"A famous plainsman was once telling a bunch of dudes about his exploits. Seems one time he was chased into a box canyon by a party of Sioux. 'Soon I was out of ammunition,' he said, 'and try as I might I couldn't climb out of that dead-end canyon.'

"'What did you do?' this one dude asked, getting more and more excited.

"'I cut my throat and died,' the plainsman replied, looking pretty sad about his terrible fate. "[12]

That man, of course, was the tall-tale master, Jim Bridger. All too frequently, as I mentioned earlier, people were too quick in judging his tales tall; many were true. In fact, some of the stories told to me as traditional lies are undeniably and demonstrably true. For example, an old-timer once mentioned to me that Lincoln, Nebraska, his home, is truly the beginning of the West. I asked him what he meant by this, why should it more than any place else be "the beginning of the west." A bit disappointed at my stupidity, he pointed out, as if to a school child, that if one stands directly in the middle of the main intersection of the main street in Lincoln, at the corner of 13th and O Streets, and faces north, everything to his left is west and everything to his right is east. Undeniable truth.

As Everett Dick, in his sensitivity for pioneer life, has pointed out in "Sunbonnet and Calico," life must have been especially tough for the pioneer woman. One of the most memorable hours of my life was spent in the Good Shepherd Home in Blair, Nebraska, listening to a weathered but unhardened old woman tell me about her arrival on these Plains. She had lived a life in Copenhagen around the turn of the century, she said, not much different from that a young woman might lead now in Lincoln or Omaha or Wichita or Sioux Falls. In the morning she got up from a comfortable bed in her nice Copenhagen apartment. She had a hot breakfast with her landlady and read the paper which had been delivered to her door. She rode the streetcar to her job in a Copenhagen business house, and in the evening she would retire to her room, where she would read by the light of a gas lamp.

But one day her brother came to her with an advertisement which had been put in the Danish newspaper by two brothers from Ord, Nebraska. They offered passage and good wages for a hired hand and a housekeeper for their ranch in the Nebraska grasslands. The brother and sister decided that the possibility offered both opportunity and adventure, and so they accepted the positions.

Upon their arrival in the United States, they rode the train to Sioux City, Iowa, for this was as far as the train went. The brothers met them and took them across the Plains in a flat-bed wagon. As the days and miles passed on their trip from civilization to the "ranch," the facts of the situation began to become painfully apparent. Tears again came to the Danish lady's eyes as she recalled the horror of the emptiness and desolation of the Plains. Finally, she said, one of the brothers said, "Here we are." But there was nothing there. Nothing.

"Where is this house I'm supposed to keep?" she asked, wondering if they were to sleep under the stars.

The brothers pointed down; they were standing atop their sod dugout. The Dane smiled as she recalled that she had cried for months at the despair of keeping house in a dirt home, "never knowing when to stop dusting."

But, she added, she had finally had her revenge on at least one of those brothers, for she had married him, and never let him forget what he had done to her young life!

One of the continual problems of Plains life was fuel. There were no trees to speak of and the crude coal from the Nebraska mines on the Missouri was too expensive to haul any distance. The universal answer was *bois de vache,* cow wood, buffalo chips. It burned hot and clean, but the humiliation of gathering the stuff plagued some women until their dying days. I once heard Everett Dick say, "Some of those ladies wore elbow length gloves for gathering fuel until their gathering days were ended. But for most, it wasn't very long before they didn't even bother to dust off their hands between stoking the stove and mixing the biscuit dough."

Manure chips were such an integral part of pioneer life that it is natural too that they found a role in pioneer story-telling. It was generally known, for example, that one bushel of buffalo chips would produce two bushels of ashes. It was this quality of "prairie oak" that gave rise to this story:

"A visitor asked a man how his family was. He replied that the children were all right but he hardly knew about his wife since theirs was a passing acquaintance. They saw each other, said he, only as she was going out with a pan of ashes and he was coming in with a bucket of cow chips, since it kept them on the go to keep from freezing. And with all that hustle and bustle, they had no time for idle visiting. "[13]

That inborn feminine revulsion toward dirt must have been considerably agitated during the years of the sod-house frontier. The wind brought dirt in at every crack, of which there were usually several, and the normal aging of the dirt houses gave rise to its share of cleaning problems:

"Until those walls were plastered, sheets were hung on the dirt walls, and house cleaning consisted of rolling up the sheets and sweeping away the cobwebs and loose dirt. My mother told me one day a rattlesnake tumbled out and coiled around the broom handle. "[14]

Although the following was said of the traditional sheep-herder's wagon cabin, the same was most certainly true also of a few sod houses:

"The wagon was swept out occasionally, and, as one herder remarked, scrubbing and dusting were done every time the Republicans swept the Solid South. "[15]

They may have differed on a lot of policy matters, but in this regard the cowboy shared the problems of the dirt farmer and the sheepherder:

"Sometimes a cowboy's clothing got pretty slick and dirty, and Pat Piper, an old cowboy, once got off a pretty good joke on Arkansas Bob about it. Pat stopped at the latter's ranch and found the whole outfit batching. The bedding was none too clean, and after Pat had gone to bed, Bob asked if there was anything else he needed. The opportunity was too good to pass up, and Pat replied: 'You might bring a shovelful of sand and throw it in the bed so I won't slip out of it.' "[16]

Buckskin and rawhide were common materials for clothing and harness on the Plains and their peculiar properties gave rise to a few stories, which again might only be extensions of the truth:

"I remember one time we had gone to town and bought a new harness for our team. It was made of buckskin and was very pretty, but we did not know that buckskin would stretch when wet. We were taking a load of coal home. A hard rain came up when we were almost home. The team kept walking but the load of coal remained stationary. When we got to the house, the wagon was a hundred yards down the road and the harness had stretched that much. We unharnessed the team and hung the harness over a post. When the sun came out the harness began to draw up by drying the buckskin and in an hour it had pulled the wagon home."[17]

A Kansan was wearing a new buckskin outfit—one that began to sag and stretch on a particularly dewy day. The hiker cut off the pieces of the legs as they flapped below his feet, but when he began to dry off, the buckskin shrank up again and he found that all he had left was "a little streak of buckskin above my knees."[18]

Some strange, inexplicable things happened on the Plains in those days. For example, a farmer who in haste loaded his gun with thumbtacks shot at a mess of blackbirds and nailed them to a huge old cottonwood tree. They eventually all flapped their wings together and flew off, tree and all.[19]

Which is reminiscent of the time some hoboes on a train enjoyed an unexpected feast when a hunter's shot scared six prairie chickens into flying against a telegraph wire, which broke their necks and flipped them into the coal car at the feet of the startled and delighted bums.[20]

All forms of transportation, from the railroad to the horse, were at one time or another the subject of tall tales. For example:

"One day a farmer and his family, living in Chase County,

started in a lumber wagon to town, which was fourteen miles away. One of the boys looked at one of the wheels so long that he became cross-eyed and they had to back up seven miles to get his eyes uncrossed. "[21]

The railroads played an important role in pioneer life, for they were the primary links with the markets and suppliers of the East. Occasionally one encounters tall tales about their phenomenal speed:

"One of these trains went so fast that the telephone poles looked like a solid board fence and when they came to a section of the country in which the fields were planted to corn and to beans alternately the whole countryside looked like succotash.

"These trains must have gone almost as fast as the one on which the brakeman was riding who had promised to kiss his girl as he rode through her hometown if she would be standing on the station platform as he went through, but the train was going so fast that he missed his girl and kissed a cow two miles down the track. "[22]

Personally, I am more inclined to believe the tall tales about the slow trains:

"The train between Holstein and Roseland ran so slow that if they coasted down hill they stopped and backed up again so they wouldn't get in ahead of schedule. "[23]

Before very long the automobile captured the imaginations of the Plainsmen just as it had everyone else's:

"A Nebraska City man . . . has invented a gasoline saver for use on his automobile. He installed one of these gas savers on his car and left town with the tank about half-full of gas. When he arrived at Falls City he had to drain the tank because it had filled up and flooded the carburetor and was making the roads muddy for the rear wheels. This man says that when the Elevator Managers' Association meets the next year he is going to drink a quart of that gasoline and he expects to make a two-hour speech in fifteen minutes. "[24]

Nor did the ever-present spirit of exaggeration diminish by

the time the airplane had been developed and was seen on the Plains; after all, lands were still being homesteaded in Nebraska well after the airplane had been developed and was in commercial use.

"Last week, about half-past ten, I saw an airplane coming straight toward our windmill. I stood there holding my breath for fear of a smash-up because it flew so close over the house that it blew all the soot down the chimney and put my fire out and then banged right for the windmill. But just before it would have hit the windmill, it stopped, backed up, and went around. Now I don't know the name of the pilot but his brakes must have been working mighty well to have stopped his plane so suddenly."[25]

As transportation improved, more and more commercial visitors came out to hawk their wares on the streets of the budding Plains towns. The medicine show was always a favorite because it had a variety of diversions in the form of musical and magic acts, pretty girls, and smooth-talking barkers. Most pioneers soon learned to be slow in accepting all of the attributes ascribed to anything sold from the backs of such wagons, but one old-timer's story suggests that at least some cures for baldness were everything they claimed to be:

"A friend of mine bought a bottle of this medicine and it was so good that one day when he accidentally spilled a little on the sidewalk he had to get a lawn mower immediately and mow the grass that took root as soon as the medicine touched the cement.

"We once knew of a cure for baldness that was so potent that it would make hair grow on the inside of the glass bottle. We spilled a little of it into a small mountain stream one day where trout were known to abound but where they were very difficult to catch. Now all anyone has to do to catch a mess of trout is to set a barber pole up beside the stream and then catch the fish when they swim up to get their hair cut."[26]

As the above story suggests, ingenious ways had to be devised to meet the unique demands of the Plains. Business schemes of the most complex and unusual nature, for example, were developed to find the best way to take advantage of the conditions offered by the Prairie environment.

"I want to tell you about my ranch right here in Lancaster County [Nebraska]. To start with, we collected about 100,000 cats. Each cat averages about 12 kittens a year. The skins run from 10 cents each for the white ones to 75 cents for the pure black. These 1,200,000 skins per year selling at an average of 35 cents each bring in a revenue of about $10,000 a day gross.

"Now, one man can skin about 60 cats per day, for $2 a day wages. It takes 100 men to operate the ranch, making the net profit for the ranch $9,800 a day.

"There is no cost for feeding because we have a rat ranch adjoining. The rats multiply about four times as fast as the cats. We started with 100,000 rats, and we have, therefore, about four rats per day for each cat, which we find to be a great plenty. We feed the rats on the carcasses of the cats after the skins have been removed and sold, giving each rat a fourth of a cat.

"The business is self-supporting; cats eat the rats, and the rats eat the cats, and we get the skins for profit. Our neighbors say it is a skin game and they can smell a rat in it some place, but we have found it to be a really satisfactory method of farming."[27]

The next story is probably the longest and most involved of the tall tales I have found in preparing this collection. Readers with weak imaginations are hereby cautioned to approach the next few paragraphs only with the greatest care:

"I was with a circus one winter in Nebraska that was different from most of the shows. The tents were made of rubber instead of canvas. The big advantage of this was that the tent could be made to fit the crowd. If a couple of fellows wanted to use it as a sleeping tent, they could put it up as a pup tent, and if the crowd at the performance was large enough, it could be stretched without limit. The center poles were glass and the glass blower would blow new ones at every town. When the show was over, all we had to do was to hit the poles with a hammer and the tent was down. The poles were hollow and we kept them full of water and let the snakes swim inside of them.

"The cook of the show served chicken every day. Now you will probably wonder how he could kill and clean chickens fast enough to serve a show troupe. First, he would place a small dynamite cap in a live chicken's mouth, then grab the chicken by the feet and swing it so as to strike its head on a wagon. This would explode the cap and kill the chicken. Then he would take a tire pump and inflate the bird until its pores would open and the feathers would fall off.

"One night we were at Woodcliffe, Nebraska, and had the largest crowd of the season. The tent was stretched six blocks long and two blocks wide and every seat was filled, while many people stood outside trying to get in.

"Our menagerie was small, as animal feed was hard to get, but we had some beaver, as all they had to [have to eat] was bark and the trained dogs with the show furnished the bark, so nothing was wasted.

"The show started off fine. The tent was lit up with large glass jugs of lightning bugs from the top. Everyone was so interested in the show that they did not notice a storm coming up. Pretty soon it started to rain and an elephant got scared and, filling his trunk with water, he blew it into the air, wetting the lightning bugs, which caused them to go out, leaving the tent in darkness. We were afraid the people would get excited and trample on one another, but almost immediately a flash of chain lightning struck the center pole and turned the snakes into electric eels which lighted the tent up as bright as day.

"The people all stayed and saw the remainder of the show and many were heard to remark that they never sat on more comfortable seats than we had in our show."[28]

Although the storm in that story saved the day, another one caused a certain amount of distress for another old-timer:

"Richard Wilson was passing the cemetery when he saw the storm approaching. He took refuge behind a large tombstone. Richard is a good truthful boy, and he told me that when the storm broke, some of his silent friends and neighbors sat up to see what the commotion was all about and when they saw it was nothing but a cyclone they lay back and said, 'My, what a refreshing breeze. Now maybe we can get a couple of hundred years of sleep.'"[29]

I have a hard time believing this next story because I am not sure whether the dead are coming back to life, as is the case in the previous tale, or whether the living are dying, or both, or neither:

"One day down in Arizona a local guide insisted that we should take a trip out to see an ancient petrified forest. After driving some time the Missus inquired about a continuous sound they were hearing, but the guide made no reply. Finally the guide stopped the car and said, 'That sound you hear is the petrified song of a petrified bird sitting on a tree in this petrified forest.'

"As the guide did not stop talking I soon discovered that he was giving us a petrified spiel and so I grabbed the wheel, but the gasoline had petrified in the tank. I carried the Missus out of the forest to a little town where I had her de-petrified."[30]

Now in the next tale our hero is only sleeping, but I place it immediately after the preceding tale on the clear evidence that one man's sleep is another man's "petrification":

"A hotel guest was much disturbed one evening by the snoring of Herman, who was sleeping in an adjoining room. Suddenly the snore ceased, and the death-like silence oppressed the listener. Thinking that something had happened to Herman, he went into his room and found him sitting up in bed.

"'I was sleeping with my mouth open,' said Herman, 'and I think I have swallowed a mouse.'

"The doctor was summoned, who called into service the hotel cat. He placed a piece of cheese some distance from the sick man's mouth, hoping that the mouse would smell the cheese, come out, and fall prey to the cat. While waiting for the plan to materialize, the doctor left the room, and Herman fell asleep and resumed his snoring. When the doctor returned, the cat was also missing."[31]

In my estimation, that tall tale comes as close as any I have seen to being no tale at all. The judges of the *Nebraska Farmer's* contest commented:

"If Herman had been snoring as loudly as the lady that James Perrin, Norfolk, told about he would have been safe. This poor soul snored so loudly that she had to get up and go into the next room to keep from waking herself up."[32]

It is increasingly obvious that even while asleep our pioneer forefathers were not safe from the dangers of the Plains. For this next story, the narrator was awarded "an aluminum handkerchief" by the editors of the *Nebraska Farmer:*

"A few nights ago my wife noticed, after she had gone to bed, that she had not removed her false teeth, and not wishing to get up to lay them away, she put them just under the mattress. The next morning we discovered we were lying on the slats; the false teeth had devoured the mattress, feather bed, and blanket."[33]

Although the next story — certainly the most incredible of this collection — did not win any prize, it did, however, receive the dubious recognition of "honorable mention" — in a lying contest, of all things!

"Congress convened and upon the advice of the President a bill was passed by both houses, without a dissenting vote, granting a bonus of $1,000 per year for the last five years to each farmer in the U.S., the money to be raised by taxes on large incomes and profits on big business. Those taxed cheerfully conceded that it was no more than the farmers' right."[34]

I hope and believe that even when the pioneer years had

passed, the people of the Plains carried with them the good humor and high hopes of the homesteaders. The following two tales suggest that this capacity for tall tales was transplanted at least into the 20th century and traveled with the Plainsmen to the European wars:

"When I was stationed in Germany during World War One we had been on the battlefield for days without any sleep. I was so very tired that I just stood up and slept. One day I was standing in a trench sleeping and it started to rain. It rained so hard that the trench filled up with water, unknown to me because I was standing there sleeping. I was sleeping so soundly that the water was up to my chin, and if I hadn't woke up just in time, I would have drowned."

"When I was stationed in Germany during World War One we had been on the battlefield for days without any sleep. I was so very tired and needed sleep. The bullets were coming at us so fast that day, but I was so tired I just lay down under a tree and went to sleep. The bullets were coming at me so hard that they kept scooping dirt up on me. And you know, I woke up just in time or I would have been buried alive."[35]

Finally, it was reported on the radio during the winter of 1969 that all scuba divers in Lincoln had been called to help locate the body of a young man who had drowned in one of the potholes so common in the city's streets, which suggests that the tall tale has survived into the era of scuba divers and paved streets.

A PARTING SHOT

7

There was, of course, no training school for the pioneer. He went out and was one or wasn't.
Mari Sandoz

"Did you hear? Fred Jensen is lying at Death's door."
"Isn't that just like old Fred! At Death's door — and still lying."
Traditional joke

How did he do it? How could he develop and maintain such a rich hoard of humor even while he was struggling for life on a land that only years before had been judged unfit for human subsistence? In working with pioneer materials, I have found that one often seeks in vain for answers from one's own understanding. Because we lack the basic information and assumptions for that logical process, it is better to ask the pioneer himself, and we are lucky to be close enough to that age to be able to find a few of the pioneers still around.

So I asked an old-timer once just how the pioneer managed to survive those early years and maintain his sense of humor. He said that perhaps it was like the dog that shinnied up a tree when a bobcat was hot on his tail: he didn't climb that tree because he could, but rather because he had to.

Did the pioneer really tell tall tales and lies? You bet he did. Although I have included in this collection the literary creations of Mari Sandoz, her work reflects and is often taken from pioneer life; the same can and must be said of the newspaper selections from popular culture; finally, a substantial number of these stories are from oral informants proper, the very pioneers who promulgated the tales.

Yes, the pioneer did his share—and more—of lying. In fact, one Nebraska farmer had such a reputation for lying, I am told, that he had to have one of his neighbors come in to call his hogs.[1]

NOTES

Introduction

1. P. J. Wyatt, "So-Called Tall Tales About Kansas," *Western Folklore* XXII:2, April 1963 (Berkeley), p. 107. All quotations from *Western Folklore* used with permission of the Regents of the University of California.

2. For example, one recent study of a tall-tale teller on Mount Desert Island, Maine contains eight stories in common with my collection. See Richard K. Lunt, "Jones Tracy: Tall-Tale Hero from Mount Desert Island," *Northeast Folklore*, X (University Press, Orno, Maine, 1969). The tales in common with this collection are: 1960M: Large Mosquitos fly off with kettle (p. 25, no. 2); 1890: The lucky shot (p. 30, no. 6); X1655. 1 Lie: the man under the hat, which is the only thing seen above the mud (pp. 35-36, no. 11); X1759 (G): Absurd disregard of the nature of gunpowder (p. 45, no. 27); X1654.5: Sharp line of demarcation between rain and clear weather (pp. 45-46, no. 28); X1796.3.1: Horses or mules pull buckboard so fast that shower fills back end of wagon or buckboard while the front stays dry (pp. 45-46, no. 28); X1651: Lie: shingling the fog (p. 28, no. 4); X1122.2: Lie: person shoots many animals with one shot (p. 31, no. 7).

3. "Champion Liar is Lied About by Liars Club," *Lincoln Star* January 2, 1970, p. 26. Used with permission of the *Lincoln Star*.

Chapter 1: Rough Weather

1. N. D. Searcy and A. R. Longwell, *Nebraska Atlas* (Nebraska Atlas Publishing Company, Kearney, 1964), pp. 11, 14.

2. Everett Dick, *The Sod-House Frontier, 1854-1890* (D. Appleton-Century, Company, New York, 1937), p. 224.

3. *Nebraska Farmer* (Lincoln), December 27, 1924. All quotations from the *Nebraska Farmer* are used with the permission of the editor.

4. Emerson Purcell, ed., *Pioneer Stories of Custer County, Nebraska* (Custer County Chief, Broken Bow, Nebraska, 1926), p. 83. All quotations from *Pioneer Stories* are used with permission of Harry Purcell.

5. *Lincoln State Journal* (Lincoln), July 5, 193? (sic), as cited by Patricia R. Jackson (Kess), "Tall Tales and Rimes of the Dust Bowl," unpublished manuscript (University of Nebraska, 1939).

6. Nebraska Federal Writers' Project news release, January 13, 1939.

7. Jackson (Kess).

8. Informant Schievelbein. For information concerning informants, see Appendix. This tale also appears in the *Nebraska Farmer*, March 14, 1925, from T. D. Scanlon.

9. Informant Schievelbein.

10. *Nebraska Farmer*, January 3, 1925, from M. J. Krebs, Antelope County.

11. Informant Hyatt.

12. Jackson (Kess), from *Lincoln State Journal*.

13. Informant Maschka.

14. Informant Schievelbein.

15. Informant Browning.

16. Informant Germolus.

17. P. J. Wyatt, "So-Called Tall Tales About Kansas," *Western Folklore* April 1963, p. 108. Informant cited as Lila Taylor.

18. Informant Harpham. Also *Nebraska Farmer*, January 10, 1925, from Jack Nelson, Boyd County.

19. Informant Dutcher.

20. Wyatt, p. 109. Informant cited as Charles Woolf.

21. Jackson (Kess), from *Lincoln State Journal*.

22. Mary Francis White, "Folktales," in *Kansas Folklore*, edited by Bill Koch and S. J. Sackett (University of Nebraska Press, Lincoln, 1961), p. 109. All quotations from *Kansas Folklore* used with permission of the University of Nebraska Press.

23. Captain Eugene F. Ware, *The Indian War of 1864* (University of Nebraska Press, Lincoln, 1911/1960), p. 56. Quotation used with permission of the University of Nebraska Press.

24. Roger L. Welsch, *Treasury of Nebraska Pioneer Folk-*

lore (University of Nebraska Press, Lincoln, 1966), pp. 157, 162-163. "Collected from the *Hastings Daily Gazette-Journal*, August 6, 1887." All quotations from *Treasury* used with permission of the University of of Nebraska Press.

25. Welsch, *Treasury*, pp. 156-158. Also *Nebraska Farmer*, March 14, 1925, from T. D. Scanlon.
26. Federal Writers' Project news release, January 13, 1939.
27. Informant Melton.
28. Welsch, *Treasury*, p. 160.
29. George L. Jackson, "Cyclone Yarns," *Prairie Schooner*, I:2, April 1927 (University of Nebraska, Lincoln), p. 158. This article also uses some material from the *Nebraska Farmer's* "Liars Lair" series.
30. Jackson, pp. 158-159.
31. Ibid., p. 160.
32. Ibid., p. 159.
33. *Nebraska Farmer,* January 3, 1925
34. Ibid.
35. Informant Dahl.
36. White, pp. 6-8. As reported in the *Osborne County Farmer*, January 20, 1916.
37. Informant Harpham; also *Nebraska Farmer*, February 14, 1925, from W. G. Besack, Chase County. A version of this tale won for W. C. Cove of Wichita, Kansas the 1959 Burlington, Wisconsin Liars Contest—probably the biggest such competition in the United States.
38. White, pp. 9-10.
39. *Nebraska Farmer*, February 14, 1925, from H. D. Lute, Keith County.
40. *Nebraska Farmer,* February 14, 1925.
41. Mari Sandoz, *Old Jules* (University of Nebraska Press, Lincoln, 1967), p. 110. All quotations from *Old Jules* are used with the permission of the University of Nebraska Press.
42. Informant Walker.
43. Informant Dutcher.
44. Anonymous informant.
45. Wyatt, p. 109. No informant cited.
46. Informant Dutcher.
47. Informant Dutcher. I was also told the same story about Sandhills lakes, that they froze so fast that they were still warm.
48. Letter in the *Portland Oregonian*, January 1951.

49. *Nebraska Farmer,* January 3, 1925, from C. B. Hope, Pawnee County.

50. *Nebraska Farmer*, January 3, 1925, Cheyenne County.

51. Informant Meines.

52. Informant Harpham.

53. *Nebraska Farmer*, January 3, 1925, Otoe County.

54. Informant Cornish.

55. *Nebraska Farmer*, January 3, 1925.

56. Unpublished Federal Writers' Project files in University of Nebraska at Omaha library.

57. Informant Schievelbein.

58. Informant Germolus. The same story appears in Wyatt, p. 110. It is worth noting that this tale was one of the most frequently received by the *Nebraska Farmer* during its 1924-1925 contest. On one occasion—December 20, 1924—the editors complained that they had received ten versions of this story in one week. On February 14, 1925, the editors said that they were receiving the story at least once a day and sometimes two or three times a day.

59. Wyatt, pp. 109-110. Informant cited as Minnie Fletcher.

60. Informant Harpham.

61. *Nebraska Farmer*, January 10, 1925.

62. Informant Harpham.

63. *Nebraska Farmer*, January 10, 1925, from Raymond Schell, Gage County.

64. Dick, *Sod-House Frontier*, p. 212.

65. Anonymous Omaha informant.

66. Informant Harpham. Also *Nebraska Farmer,* January 10, 1925, from Helen Hanson, Thurston County, as it had happened in Kansas.

67. *Nebraska Farmer,* December 12, 1924.

68. *Nebraska Farmer*, January 31, 1925.

69. *Nebraska Farmer*, March 14, 1925, from Hans Hansen, Red Willow County.

70. Anonymous informant.

71. Informant Fairchild.

72. Informant Thompson.

73. Anonymous informant in Byron, Nebraska.

74. Wyatt, p. 107. Collected by Frances Normandin. Also informant Meines.

75. Thomas Henry Tibbles, *Buckskin and Blanket Days* (Doubleday, Garden City, 1905/1957), p. 223.

76. Informant Roy. Also *Nebraska Farmer*, January 31,

1925, from C. F. Kyle, Superior, Nebraska.

77. Informant Harpham.
78. Anonymous informant. A story of this same kind appears in *Kansas Folklore*, White, p. 10.
79. Wyatt, p. 108. Informant John Glover.
80. White, pp. 8-9.
81. Informant Harpham. Also *Nebraska Farmer*, December 27, 1924, from Herluff Pederson, St. Paul, Nebraska.
82. Mark L. Felber, in *The Wingfoot Clan* (Lincoln), September 24, 1948.
83. *Nebraska Farmer*, March 14, 1925, from T. D. Scanlon, Boone County.
84. *Nebraska Farmer*, February 28, 1925, from Elsie Hubbard, Logan County.
85. Informant Rhea.
86. *Nebraska Farmer*, December 27, 1924, from H. T. Weerts, Meadow Grove.
87. Welsch, *Treasury*, p. 159.
88. Wyatt, p. 108. Collected by Lila Taylor.
89. Informant Harpham.
90. Sandoz, *Old Jules*, p. 149.
91. *Nebraska Farmer*, January 3, 1925, from W. H. Bruner, Hall County.
92. Anonymous Byron, Nebraska informant.

Chapter 2: Fabulous Land

1. Everett Dick, *Vanguards of the Frontier* (D. Appleton-Century, Co., New York, 1941), p. 250.
2. Rufus Sage, *Rocky Mountain Life* (Boston, 1857), as cited by Merrill Mattes, in *The Great Platte River Road* (Nebraska State Historical Society, Lincoln, 1969), p. 423.
3. John A. MacMurphy, "Part of the Making of a Great State," *Proceedings and Collections of the Nebraska State Historical Society,* I:1 (Nebraska State Historical Society, Lincoln, 1894), p. 15-16.
4. Roger L. Welsch, *Treasury of Nebraska Pioneer Folklore*, p. 29.
5. Eugene F. Ware, *The Indian War of 1864*, pp. 225-226.
6. N. D. Searcy and A. R. Longwell, *Nebraska Atlas*, p. 18.
7. Anonymous Omaha informant.
8. Mary Francis White, "Folktales," in *Kansas Folklore,* edited by Bill Koch and S. J. Sackett, p. 18.

9. Mattes, p. 373
10. Ibid., p. 392.
11. Kirk Anderson, "Trip to Utah, 1858," edited by Robert T. Wells, *Missouri Historical Society Bulletin*, XVIII (October, 1961), p. 9; used with permission of the Society.
12. Cornelius Conway, *The Utah Expedition* (Cincinnati, 1858), as cited by Mattes, pp. 404-405.
13. Lewis B. Daugherty, "Experiences . . . on the Oregon Trail," edited by Ethel Withers, *Missouri Historical Review*, (April, July, October, 1930; January, April, 1931), as cited by Mattes, p. 294.
14. Also *Nebraska Farmer*, February 14, 1925, from H.G. McClintoch, Pawnee County.
15. *Nebraska Farmer*, February 14, 1925, from Mrs. Dora Farmenski, Boone County.
16. Informant Lafferty.
17. *Nebraska Farmer*, February 14, 1925.
18. Ibid.
19. Ibid.
20. Ibid., from Mrs. Dora Farmenski.
21. *Nebraska Farmer*, February 7, 1925.
22. Informant Ragan.
23. Informant Larkowski, as the story used to be told by an old timer from around Nysted and Dannebrog.
24. *Nebraska Farmer*, March 21, 1925, from W. O. Whitehead.
25. Informant Harpham.
26. *Nebraska Farmer*, January 3, 1925, William E. Steele, Brown County.
27. Federal Writers' Project news release, June 9, 1939, by J. H. Norris, who said, "This is the exact conversation as nearly as I can remember it as related to me by A. D. Jillson of Springview, Nebraska in 1896." A similar tale won the 1957 Burlington, Wisconsin Liars Contest for Albert Hopkins of Madison; he told the tale, however, as having happened in South Dakota.
28. Everett Dick, *The Sod-House Frontier*, p. 6.
29. Mark Twain, *Roughing It* (American Publishing Co., Hartford, 1886), p. 21.
30. Ibid., p. 60.
31. D. A. Shaw, *Eldorado, or California As Seen by a Pioneer* (Los Angeles, 1900), as cited by Mattes, p. 58.
32. Anonymous informant.
33. Informant Welsch.

34. Anonymous Omaha informant.
35. Mari Sandoz, *The Tom-Walker* (Dial Press, New York, 1947), p. 292.
36. Dick, *Sod-House Frontier*, pp. 42-44. Speaking of eager-but-innocent buyers who found no towns and no trees on the Plains, this seems as good a place as any, and probably the best, to remind the reader of the 19th-century slogan, "Rain follows the plow"—one of the briefest Plains lies known, but an idea long-lived and horrendously influential in the lives of thousands of conned folk. The idea was simply that the slogan was literally true. As Charles Dana Wilber (who coined the phrase, but not the idea) said: "The plow was the avant courier . . . In the sweat of his face, toiling with his hands, man can persuade the heavens to yield their treasures of dew and rain upon the land he has chosen for his dwelling place." To break the sod, to plant trees, to lay rails, to string telegraph wires—these acts, *in and of themselves*, would change the weather patterns of the Plains and bring down the rains. Though the pioneers could hardly laugh at this man-made aspect of their dream deferred, we today can perhaps be allowed a wry chuckle over the rain-follows-the-plow motif. The story of this 19th-century phenomenon was succinctly told over two decades ago by Henry Nash Smith in his *Virgin Land;* see especially Chapter XVI, "The Garden and the Desert," from which the Wilber quote is taken. A more recent and detailed study is David M. Emmons' *Garden in the Grasslands: Boomer Literature of the Central Great Plains* (University of Nebraska Press, Lincoln, 1971).
37. Dick, *Sod-House Frontier*, p. 41.
38. Welsch, *Treasury,* p. 161.
39. As cited by John D. Hicks in *The Populist Revolt* (University of Nebraska Press, Lincoln, 1963).
40. Roger L. Welsch, *Sod Walls: The Story of the Nebraska Sod House* (Purcells, Broken Bow, 1967), p. 183. Quotations from *Sod Walls* are used with permission of Harry Purcell.
41. Informant Dutcher.
42. White, pp. 12-13.
43. Ibid., pp. 17-18.
44. *Nebraska Farmer,* January 31, 1925, from M. E. Nel-

son, Howe. The McKelvie bull does appear again (see Chapter 4, "Livestock" section), but we never learn *how* he rescued Mr. Nelson.

45. *Nebraska Farmer,* February 14, 1925, Mrs. Edward Duering.
46. *Nebraska Farmer,* February 14, 1925.
47. *Nebraska Farmer,* February 21, 1925.
48. *Nebraska Farmer,* March 21, 1925, from D. D. Jansen, obviously of York County.
49. White, pp. 19-20.
50. Welsch, *Treasury,* pp. 152-154.
51. White, p. 17.
52. Ibid., p. 19.
53. Informant Dewey.

Chapter 3: Big Men

1. Louise Pound, *Nebraska Folklore* (University of Nebraska Press, Lincoln, 1959), pp. 124-125.
2. Paul R. Beath, *Febold Feboldson: Tall Tales From the Great Plains* (University of Nebraska Press, Lincoln, 1948).
3. Roger L. Welsch, "Populism and Folklore," *Kansas Quarterly,* I:4, Fall 1969 (Manhattan), p. 117.
4. Stanley Vestal, *Jim Bridger, Mountain Man* (William Morrow and Co., New York, 1946), p. 137.
5. Gene Caesar, *King of the Mountain Men: The Life of Jim Bridger* (E. P. Dutton, New York, 1961), p. 82.
6. Ibid., pp. 134, 82.
7. Ibid., pp. 14, 13.
8. Mari Sandoz, *The Tom-Walker,* p. 32.
9. Ibid., p. 83.
10. Ibid., p. 92.
11. Ibid., p. 99.
12. For example, see Lunt's study of Jones Tracy (supra, Introduction, note #2), which traces precisely this kind of hero development.
13. Sandoz, *The Tom-Walker,* p. 114.
14. Ibid., p. 105.
15. Ibid., p. 117.
16. Ibid., p. 276.

17. Ibid., p. 327.

18. Ibid., p. 282.

19. For further information about Antoine Barada and Moses Stocking, see Louise Pound, "Nebraska Strong Men," in *Nebraska Folklore* pp. 122-143; and Welsch, *Treasury,* pp. 171-175.

20. Informant Zurleen provided all the Melcher tales; further inquiries in the area have produced no further tales.

21. Solomon D. Butcher, *Pioneer History of Custer County, Nebraska* (Sage Books, Denver, 1965), pp. 42-43. Quotations used with permission of Harry E. Chrisman.

22. Informant Chamberlain.

23. "Days Gone By," *Crete* (Nebraska) *News,* January, 1970.

24. Welsch, *Treasury,* p. 161.

25. Informant Mohatt. This tale won honorable mention in the 1948 Burlington, Wisconsin Liars Contest.

26. Undated letter to the editor, *Omaha World-Herald.*

27. Informant Harpham.

28. *Nebraska Farmer,* December 20, 1924.

29. Informant McKillip.

30. *Nebraska Farmer,* March 14, 1925.

31. Ibid., January 24, 1925, from Jack Dempcy of Moorefield.

32. Federal Writers' Project news release, September 9, 1940, Omaha; by Hart Jenks; from *Omaha Daily Bee,* October 5, 1890.

33. Federal Writers' Project news release, August 5, 1940; by Hart Jenks; from *Omaha Daily Bee,* October 10, 1890.

34. *Nebraska Farmer,* February 7, 1925, from M. D. Anderson, Bradshaw.

35. Informant Haney.

36. Informant Dutcher.

37. Anonymous Lincoln informant.

38. Informant Harpham.

39. Letter to the editor, *Omaha World-Herald.* See also *Kansas Folklore,* White, p. 16.

40. Informant Cox. Given as "Oliver Swick's Song," entered in a *Custer County Chief* tall-tale contest.

41. Informant Collier.

42. I have no idea where I first heard this story other than that it was somewhere in Nebraska.

43. Martha Dirks, "Teen-Age Folklore from Kansas," *Western Folklore,* XXII:2, April 1963 (Berkeley), p. 100, #165.
44. Butcher, pp. 82-83.
45. Dirks, p. 100, #165.

Chapter 4: Strange Critters

1. For a history of the phrase, see J. Rea, "Seeing the Elephant," *Western Folklore,* January 1969, pp. 21-26.
2. Merrill Mattes, *The Great Platte River Road,* pp. 61-62.
3. Sandoz, *The Tom-Walker,* p. 306.
4. Ibid., p. 123-124.
5. Louise Pound, *Nebraska Folklore,* pp. 114-116.
6. Sandoz, *Old Jules,* pp. 412-413.
7. Mary Francis White, "Folktales," in *Kansas Folklore,* edited by Bill Koch and S. J. Sackett, pp. 10-11; and several Nebraska informants.
8. Informant Harpham.
9. Informant Cooley.
10. Federal Writers' Project news release, August 26, 1940; by Hart Jenks; from *Omaha Weekly Bee,* January 27, 1875.
11. Ibid.
12. *Nebraska Farmer,* January 3, 1925, from C. H. Little, Dodge County.
13. *Nebraska Farmer,* January 31, 1925.
14. *Nebraska Farmer,* April 18, 1925, from anonymous writer, Antelope County.
15. *Nebraska Farmer,* January 31, 1925.
16. Informant McGaughey.
17. Federal Writers' Project news release, January 13, 1939.
18. *Nebraska Farmer,* February 7, 1925, from Leopold Moller, Fremont.
19. *Nebraska Farmer,* April 18, 1925, from Adam Hofferher, Madison County.
20. Informant Dutcher.
21. White, pp. 11-12.
22. Mattes, p. 250.
23. *Nebraska Farmer,* February 7, 1925.
24. P. J. Wyatt, "So-Called Tall Tales About Kansas," *Western Folklore,* April 1963, pp. 110-111.

25. Informant Harpham. It is interesting that this is the only etymological tall tale I have encountered from traditional or quasi-traditional sources, whereas they are a dominant element of the Febold Feboldson cycle.
26. Wyatt, p. 110.
27. *Nebraska Farmer,* February 7, 1925, from William Lintelman, Gresham.
28. Wyatt, p. 109. From Leona Wells.
29. Wyatt, p. 110. Informant Bernice Dunlop.
30. Informant Dutcher.
31. Thomas Henry Tibbles, *Buckskin and Blanket Days,* p. 125.
32. Informant Schievelbein.
33. Wyatt, pp. 107-108. Collected by Lila Taylor.
34. *Nebraska Farmer,* March 7, 1925.
35. Informant Dady.
36. *Nebraska Farmer,* February 14, 1925.
37. White, p. 14.
38. Roger L. Welsch, "Sweet Nebraska Land" (Folkways Recordings, FH5337; New York, 1964), brochure.
39. *Nebraska Farmer,* January 17, 1925, from Lawrence Russell, Orleans, et al.
40. Anonymous informant.
41. Informant Lafferty.
42. *Nebraska Farmer,* February 14, 1925, from Joseph Zvolanek, Saline County.
43. Emerson Purcell, ed., *Pioneer Stories of Custer County,* pp. 65-66.
44. Informant Schievelbein.
45. Mark Twain, *Roughing It,* pp. 31-33.
46. *Nebraska Farmer,* March 21, 1925, from E. A. Blumenthal, Webster County.
47. Informant Nelson.
48. *Nebraska Farmer,* January 24, 1925, from Herman Neiman, Curtis.
49. Informant Kloefkorn.
50. Solomon D. Butcher, *Pioneer History of Custer County,* p. 134.
51. This coyote story is from Mark Twain's *Roughing It,* pp. 48-53. At this point in the text I use the name Samuel L. Clemens, rather than his better known pseudonym. The reason may seem like a tall tale itself. Mrs. Helen Lane, Permissions Editor at Harper & Row, Publishers, writes:

Mark Twain is a registered trademark, and when it is used, we are required by the trustees for the estate to ask a nominal charge. . . . This would apply only when you are quoting at some length from public domain material and not to passages under 500 words. If you do not care to pay for the trademark when quoting beyond 500 words, simply use the author's real name, Samuel L. Clemens. [letters to author, January 30, 1970 and September 20, 1971]

I cannot help but think what cynically caustic words Mark Twain would have penned about this exploitation of his name!

52. Informant Harpham; an extended version of the same story appears in White, p. 14.
53. Welsch, *Treasury,* pp. 46-48.
54. Welsch, *Sod Walls,* pp. 177-179.
55. Anonymous Lincoln informant.
56. *Nebraska Farmer,* April 11, 1925, from Emil Peter, Colfax County.
57. Anonymous Omaha informant.
58. Everett Dick, *Sod House Frontier,* pp. 204-205.
59. James C. Olson, *History of Nebraska* (University of Nebraska Press, Lincoln, 1966), pp. 174-175.
60. Federal Writers' Project news release, August 26, 1940; by Hart Jenks; from *Omaha Weekly Bee,* September 30, 1874.
61. For an example of this tale, see Welsch, *Treasury,* p. 136.
62. Sandoz, *Son of the Gamblin' Man: The Youth of an Artist* (Clarkson Potter, New York, 1960), p. 122.
63. Fannie McCormick, *A Kansas Forum* (John F. Alden, New York, 1891), p. 76.
64. White, p. 22.
65. White, p. 18.
66. Informant Harpham.

Chapter 5: Hard Times

1. Welsch, *Treasury,* p. 46.
2. Everett Dick, *Vanguards of the Frontier,* p. 403.
3. Dick, *Sod-House Frontier,* p. 182.

4. Dick, *Vanguards of the Frontier,* p. 317. Twain tells much the same story in *Roughing It,* except that the main dish in his version is mackerel.
5. Welsch, "Populism and Folklore," *Kansas Quarterly,* Fall 1969, p. 114.
6. Informant Schneider.
7. Sandoz, *The Tom-Walker,* p. 123.
8. Informant Boker.
9. Informant Harpham.
10. Informant Boker.
11. *Nebraska Farmer,* February 14, 1925, from D. D. Jansen of York County and F. J. Clark of Merrick County.
12. Informant Harpham.
13. Informant Harpham.
14. Mary Francis White, "Folktales," in *Kansas Folklore,* edited by Bill Koch and S. J. Sackett, pp. 22-23.

Chapter 6: Other Plains Lies

1. Everett Dick, *Sod-House Frontier,* p. 35.
2. Welsch, "Populism and Folklore," p. 115.
3. Emerson Purcell, ed., *Pioneer Stories of Custer County, Nebraska,* p. 66. This and the following tale are from the talented pen of George Mair of the *Callaway Courier.*
4. Purcell, p. 167.
5. Anonymous Lincoln informant.
6. Informant Farmer.
7. Dick, *Sod-House Frontier,* p. 166.
8. Welsch, *Treasury,* pp. 160-161.
9. Sandoz, *Old Jules,* p. 132.
10. Twain, *Roughing It,* p. 73.
11. Mark Twain uses a similar story in *Roughing It,* p. 76. His stage driver nearly starved because he had been rendered so leaky by bullet holes that "he couldn't hold his vittles." Twain adds, however, "This person's statements were not generally believed."
12. Informant Haney. Much the same story appears in the *Nebraska Farmer,* December 20, 1924, from Fern Bunker, Humphrey. The story, incidentally, won for Bunker a "concrete accordion"; this version has the frontiersman

NOTES   *151*

trapped on a ledge with a bear — he "just sat there and let the bear eat him up."

13. Everett Dick, "Sunbonnet and Calico, the Homesteader's Consort," *Nebraska History,* 47:1 March, 1966 (Lincoln), p. 6. This tale from Kathryne Lichty's unpublished dissertation, "A History of the Settlement of the Nebraska Sand Hills," University of Wyoming, 1960.
14. Informant Wood.
15. Dick, *Vanguards of the Frontier,* p. 500.
16. Ibid., p. 492.
17. Informant Dutcher. Another version of the same tale appears in Welsch, *Treasury,* p. 159, and another in the *Nebraska Farmer,* December 20, 1924.
18. Mary Francis White, "Folktales," in *Kansas Folklore,* edited by Bill Koch and S. J. Sackett, p. 10.
19. White, p. 13. The universality of these tales was demonstrated to me dramatically while working on this very tale. On the day I was typing the manuscript for this very page, I received a letter from an English friend of mine, whom I had told only that I was working on tall tales. He wrote me a version of this story almost identical with the text printed here. He remarked that it is a common tale in the region of his home.
20. Welsch, *Treasury,* p. 160.
21. *Nebraska Farmer,* March 7, 1925, from Clifford J. Brown, Cass County.
22. *Nebraska Farmer,* March 7, 1925, from Lyle Hiatt, Jefferson County.
23. Informant Harpham.
24. *Nebraska Farmer,* March 7, 1925, from George C. Holscher, Otoe County.
25. *Nebraska Farmer,* March 7, 1925, from Mrs. John Nichols, Butler County.
26. *Nebraska Farmer,* April 18, 1925, from Ralph Reed, Hamilton County.
27. *Nebraska Farmer,* May 16, 1925, from M. L. Johnson, Lancaster County. The last tale to appear in the "Liars Lair" series of the *Nebraska Farmer.*
28. *Nebraska Farmer,* March 14, 1925, from Merle E. Monroe.
29. *Nebraska Farmer,* March 14, 1925.

30. *Nebraska Farmer,* April 11, 1925, from H. D. Lute, Keith County.
31. *Nebraska Farmer,* January 3, 1925, from Irene I. Caldwell, Swanton.
32. *Nebraska Farmer,* January 3, 1925, from James Perrin, Norfolk.
33. *Nebraska Farmer,* January 17, 1925, from Jurgen Aden, Gothenburg.
34. *Nebraska Farmer,* January 10, 1925, from Mrs. L. Cornwell, Boone County.
35. These two tales are from informant Larkowski; they were originally told by "the father of a man whom we knew that lived near Nysted."

Chapter 7: A Parting Shot

1. Anonymous informant. Also *Nebraska Farmer,* December 20, 1924, from J. R. Kelly, of Salem, Nebraska.

APPENDIX: INFORMANTS

To everyone else the label "informant" carries ominous and suspicious meanings, but to us folklorists the term is the very foundation of folklore studies; it is he who provides the raw data with which folklorists work, the folklore.

My contacts with these informants have been brief, and frequently only through the mails, so I am not able to give biographical data about them. But I suspect that many of them developed their repertoire of tales in much the same way as Ray Harpham, from Holstein, Nebraska, one of my best story sources.

He closed one of his letters, "I will try and come up with some more of the tall tales I heard as a boy about 1915 or so. I love to remember the men who told them. They were some real characters, and tales of blizzards, droughts, anything that happened usually found first telling in my Uncle's Blacksmith Shop."

In a letter he gave another hint where he, as a boy, learned the tale-smith's art: "Most of the ones that stick with me I heard from my uncles. There were six of them and after Sunday dinner they would gather in the feed alley of the barn and whittle and yarn. It was a custom for them to whistle a tune till a story was told but I'm sure they were all thinking of the next one."

I am listing these names, therefore, to give proper credit for these stories and to offer my thanks to each of them for their kind help.

Harold Boker, Omaha
Mrs. Dora Browning, Falls City
Sherry Chamberlin, Mason City
Harry E. Chrisman, Denver, Colorado

Mamie Collier, Dunning
Mrs. Dale Cooley, Broken Bow
James Cornish, Oconto
Lizzie Cox, Brewster
Mrs. Guy Dady, Broken Bow
Sam Dahl, Lincoln
Irene Dewey, Spencer
Robert Dutcher, Omaha
Warren Fairchild, Lincoln
Jim Farmer, Broken Bow
Paul Germolus, Omaha
Ned O. Haney, Macomb, Illinois
Ray Harpham, Holstein
Ed Henry, East Lansing, Michigan
Ellis Hyatt, Ansley
Bill Kloefkorn, Lincoln
Mrs. Vernon T. Lafferty, McCook
The Rev. Lavern Larkowski, Gretna
Mrs. A. S. Maschka, Omaha
Mrs. Kathryn McGauhey, Wheatridge, Colorado
G. McKillip, Milburn
M. K. Meines, Harrison, Arkansas
Mrs. Don Melton, Naponee
Charles J. Mohatt, Broken Bow
Mrs. Jim Nelson, Broken Bow
Clyde Ragan, Omaha
Vivian Rhea, Omaha
Louis Roy, Fremont
H. E. Schievelbein, Arapahoe
F. H. Schneider, Krell
The Rev. Bill Thompson, Blair
James Walker, Bruning
Chris Welsch, Lincoln
Myrtle Wood, Wabash
Paul B. Zurleen, Columbus

Folklore field work is a continuing process and even when a large enough body of materials has been assembled for a reliable sample or publication, the folklorist knows that he does not have every possible item. I am still looking for tall tales, therefore, and I would welcome letters or calls from any readers who might be willing to share their Plains tall tales with me, as the kind persons listed above have.

Roger Welsch
Nebraska Wesleyan University
Lincoln, Nebraska

ACKNOWLEDGMENTS

The quotation by Marianne Moore on page 120 is from her *The Pangolin* (©1941, 1969 by Marianne Moore, published by The Macmillan Co., New York).

When permission was requested to use the illustration on page 42, we received the following letter:

CREATIVE
SERVICES

Mr. Durrett Wagner, Editor
The Swallow Press Incorporated
1139 South Wabash Avenue
Chicago, Illinois 60605

Dear Mr. Wagner:

Anybody who would publish a book called SHINGLING THE THE FOG AND OTHER PLAINS LIES can't be all bad. And, it would indeed be some sort of an honor to have one of our posters illustrating such a tome. Therefore, permission is hereby granted for you to reproduce the " Ski Nebraska" poster in your upcoming book, with certain provisions, of course.

Quite naturally, the highly intricate art which graces this poster is worth a good deal of money, possibly even approaching the six figure class. Its value becomes even more apparent when it must indeed be the only illustration to carry the reader happily through some 150 pages of typography reeking with prevarication. " Fabulous Land" indeed!

Yet, in the interest of American literature's future and because we couldn't be all bad either, we shall not hold you up on the price. Certainly not. But the least you could do is send us a half dozen complimentary copies of the book which we will judiciously sow, so as to further stimulate sales hereabouts.

Now then, kindly use this credit line, preferably on the page opposite the poster repreduction so as not to mar the glorious graphic effect:

The incredibly magnificent landscape and message on the facing page is a reproduction from a poster series published by Creative Services of Denver. Copyright 1971. Reprinted with permission. The series is called The Great ImPosters and includes Ski Lubbock, Ski Kansas, Ski Iowa, Ski Burbank, Ski D.C., and Fish Salt Lake, all with appropriate illustration on exquisite paper. Posters may be ordered from Creative Services, 100 Garfield, Denver 80206, at 50¢ wholesale, $1 retail plus freight. When ordering, please specify at least a dozen posters. After all, it's the least you can do since the reprint permission didn't cost this book publisher a cent. By the by, to save the freight charges, send a stamped self-addressed tube when ordering. Thank you.

MOTIF INDEX

In an effort to make this collection useful as well as entertaining, I include a motif index, based on Stith Thompson's *Motif-Index of Folk-Literature* (Indiana University Press, Bloomington, 1966). The motif numbers and headings here are Thompson's. All the lies and tall tales in *Shingling the Fog* are not indexed—only those which correspond to Thompson's *Motif-Index*.